TERRORISM FUTURES

Front Cover Image: Screen shot at the 0:26 second mark from a propaganda video of a remote controlled machine gun fielded by Ajnad al-Sham Islamic Union, Damascus, Syria in March 2014. Source: "سي يك يب شاشر عينصت نيدهاجملا يدبأ بلع بلاعت هلال لضفب مت". *YouTube* (Ajnad al-Sham Islamic Union video posting). 20 March 2014, https://www.youtube.com/watch?v=vHz19XM5Cg8. 1:30 Minutes. [For Public Distribution/No Restrictions on Use]

TERRORISM FUTURES

Evolving Technology and TTPs Use

Robert J. Bunker

Foreword by Rohan Gunaratna

A C/O Futures Pocketbook

To order additional copies of this book, contact:
Xlibris
844-714-8691
www.Xlibris.com
Orders@Xlibris.com
818051

CONTENTS

The following essays originally appeared in:

Essay 1. *TRENDS Research & Advisory*. Terrorism Futures Series. 14 December 2014, http://trendsinstitution.org/?p=762.

Essay 2. *TRENDS Research & Advisory*. Terrorism Futures Series. 11 January 2015, http://trendsinstitution.org/?p=870.

Essay 3. *TRENDS Research & Advisory*. Terrorism Futures Series. 10 February 2015, http://trendsinstitution.org/?p=1004.

Essay 4. *TRENDS Research & Advisory*. Terrorism Futures Series. 18 March 2015, http://trendsinstitution.org/close-to-the-body-and-body-cavity-suicide-bombs/.

Essay 5. *TRENDS Research & Advisory*. Terrorism Futures Series. 21 April 2015, http://trendsinstitution.org/?p=1110.

Essay 6. *TRENDS Research & Advisory*. Terrorism Futures Series. 21 June 2015, http://trendsinstitution.org/?p=1250.

Essay 7. *TRENDS Research & Advisory*. Terrorism Futures Series. 10 August 2015, http://trendsinstitution.org/?p=1358.

Essay 8. *TRENDS Research & Advisory*. Terrorism Futures Series. 2 February 2016, http://trendsinstitution.org/?p=1692.

Essay 9. *TRENDS Research & Advisory*. Terrorism Futures Series. 14 June 2017, http://trendsinstitution.org/laptop-bombs-and-civil-aviation-terrorism-potentials-and-carry-on-travel-bans/.

About C/O Futures, LLC

C/◈Futures
Counter-OPFOR

C/O Futures, LLC is a small business, located by the renowned Claremont Colleges consortium, that provides specialized research and analytical consulting services that facilitate client knowledge solutions for addressing future socio-political and operational environment shaping and response.

Our corporate mission is to further and protect liberal-democratic values and institutions—both public and private—in the face of disruptive systemic level change taking place during the transition from the modern to post-modern epochs of human civilization.

Our consulting services range from the tactical though the grand strategic levels of interactions. One major focus of these services pertains to the broadening spectrum of **threat groups**—ranging from more evolved forms of gangs though authoritarian regimes with increased global capacity— now actively challenging liberal-democratic governance both domestically and abroad. Other service areas concern

technology and **concepts**, both individually and interactively. Residing at the tactical and operational levels, these areas seek to characterize generic and specific threat group utilization of technology (and the concepts supporting such use) as well as the novel use of standalone concepts and to develop countermeasures and defensive response protocols against them. Our services also facilitate capitalizing on advanced technology & concepts for policy and operational overmatch purposes.

Another client service area pertains to **narratives** vis-a-vis both constructed realities and cultural norms related to threat groups and the response for deradicalization and counter-narrative purposes. A final service area concerns the process and effects of **epochal change** pertaining to the national strategic through civilizational levels of global activities and interactions. All C/O Futures, LLC research is influenced through the lens of the epochal change construct developed in the later 1980s (by one of its principals) in order to preserve liberal-democratic values and institutions through the global civilizational transition period underway.

To view C/O Futures, LLC research products and strategic consultancy services see: https://www.cofutures.net.

Acronyms

3D	Three Dimensional
4D	Four Dimensional
ADS	Active Denial System
AFV	Armored Fighting Vehicle
AI	Artificial Intelligence
AKA	Also Known As
AP	Armor Piercing
APC	Armored Personnel Carrier
AQAP	Al Qaida in the Arabian Peninsula
ATF	Bureau of Alcohol, Tobacco, Firearms, and Explosives
AVBIED	Armored Vehicle Borne Improvised Explosive Device
BCB	Body Cavity Bomb
BRT	Bond-Relationship Targeting
C	Cyber
C2	Command and Control

CBR	Chemical, Biological, and Radiological
CBRN	Chemical, Biological, Radiological, and Nuclear
CBRNE	Chemical, Biological, Radiological, Nuclear, and Explosive
CD	Compact Disc
CI	Confidential Informant
CJNG	Cártel de Jalisco Nueva Generación (Jalisco New Generation Cartel)
CNC	Computer Numerical Control
CONOPS	Concept of Operations
COVID-19	Coronavirus Disease 2019
CSRL	Cártel Santa Rosa de Lima (Santa Rosa de Lima Cartel)
DARPA	Defense Advanced Research Projects Agency
DHS	Department of Homeland Security
DNA	Deoxyribonucleic Acid
DoS	Denial-of-Service
EU	European Union
FBI	Federal Bureau of Investigation
FBIS	Foreign Broadcast Information Service
FLIR	Forward Looking Infrared
FPS	First Person Shooter
FPS	First Person Stabber or Slasher [Variant]
FSA	Free Syrian Army
G8	The Group of Eight
GPS	Global Positioning System

GPT	Generative Pre-trained Transformer
H	Hyper
HAZMAT	Hazardous Materials
HIV	Human Immunodeficiency Virus
HMMWV	High Mobility Multipurpose Wheeled Vehicle; Humvee
HPM	High-Power Microwave
I&W	Indications & Warnings
IED	Improvised Explosive Device
IFTT	If This, Then That
IRA	Irish Republican Army
IS	Islamic State
ISIS	Islamic State in Iraq and Syria
ISR	Intelligence, Surveillance, and Reconnaissance
IV	Intravenous
JT	Just Terror
LASER	Light Amplification by Stimulated Emission of Radiation
LAX	Los Angeles International Airport
LTTE	Liberation Tigers of Tamil Eelam
MNF	Multinational Force
NGO	Non-Governmental Organization
OICW	Objective Individual Combat Weapon

OODA	Observe-Orient-Decide-Act
OSJ	Open Source Jihad
OSM	Mosul International Airport
PGF	Precision Guided Firearm
PIN	Personal Identification Number
PKK	Partiya Karkerên Kurdistanê (Kurdistan Workers' Party)
PTSD	Post-Traumatic Stress Disorder
RCS	Radar Cross Section
RFW	Radio Frequency Weapon
RPG	Rocket Propelled Grenade
SOA	Soldier(s) of Allah
SUV	Sport Utility Vehicle
SWAT	Special Weapon and Tactics
SynBio	Synthetic Biology
T	Time
TATP	Triacetone Triperoxide
TSA	Transportation Security Administration
TTP(s)	Tactics, Techniques and Procedures
UAE	United Arab Emirates
UAS	Unmanned Aerial System
UAV	Unmanned Aerial Vehicle
US	United States
USA	United States of America
USB	Universal Serial Bus

VBIED	Vehicle Borne Improvised Explosive Device
VIP	Very Important Person
VR	Virtual Reality
WHIM	What-If Machine
WTO	World Trade Organization
X	Line Space
X, Y	Plane Space
X, Y, Z	Cube Space
YPG	Yekîneyên Parastina Gel (The People's Defense Units; Kurdish)

Foreword

Terrorist Imagineering

Rohan Gunaratna

Singapore

7 October 2020

Understanding the Operating Environment

Like the invention of the atom bomb, explosives, and the machine gun changed warfare dramatically, terrorist inventions and innovations changed the global threat landscape forever. With the integration of human beings willing to kill and die in terrorism and guerrilla attacks, the nature of the threat changed. Today, the largest number of terrorist fatalities and casualties stem from suicide attacks, both vehicle- and human-borne. In the lead up to al Qaeda's landmark attacks on September 11, 2001, I wrote of the emerging suicide threat in an article titled, "Suicide Terrorism: A Global Threat," published in *Jane's Intelligence Review* in April 2000. Some of my peers, who could not believe that people want to die killing others, claimed that I had exaggerated the threat. After the 9/11 attacks killed 2,977 people, the largest number of people to perish in one attack, there was shock and grief. There was also an acknowledgement that suicide terrorism is an apex security threat worldwide.

One of the foremost experts on terrorist invention and innovation, Robert Bunker examines how technological trends intersect with and influence future threats. Anyone reading Dr. Bunker's study will also ask whether he has assessed the threat accurately. Forecasting threats, predicting trends and patterns, requires an appreciable understanding of the environment and a deep knowledge of threat entities. Having studied the evolving threat landscape for over two decades, Dr. Bunker seeks to address the American challenge. The 9/11 Commissioners described it as the "failure of imagination." To stay ahead of the threat, national security practitioners and counter terrorism scholars grapple with this challenge every day.

How is Terrorism Changing?

Are threat groups still seeking to acquire Weapons of Mass Destruction and other sophisticated weapons, or are they devolving to a simpler tactical approach using bladed weapons and vehicles? The security and intelligence community is trying to determine if terrorist and other violent non-state actors are technophile radical innovators, seamlessly identifying and deploying new technologies to their cause or if they returning to a simpler tactical range. Have the security and intelligence services forced them to become cautious modifiers of existing technologies and lesser sophistication to lower their signature? The answer would seem obvious. Although there are exceptions, the world's deadliest two movements, the Islamic State and al Qaeda, are radical innovators. They control territory and have access to intellectual and financial resources. These groups seek to undermine and destroy the existing socio-political system as well as existing social norms to advance their ends. Conversely, other analysts and scholars argue that terrorists and other violent non-state actors are conservative goal seeking maximisers, who adhere to well-known tactics, targets and procedures because they know what works. In general, violent non-state actors tend to use lower sophisticated operational means and tactics. Nonetheless, certain high-tech headways arguably offer them handy and cheap ways to rationalise their workflows. They include 3D printers, unmanned aerial vehicles (UAVs), social media technologies and bots, which together with remote controlled firearms, offer both defensive and offensive capabilities for terrorists. We have witnessed several incidents underlining that threat groups are eager to take advantage of these beneficial novelties. The act of challenging powerful states is fraught enough that evolving their existing tactics, targets and procedures is the only way these groups have a chance to survive, let alone achieve their ends. This debate has profound implications; the 9/11 Commission highlighted this when it stated the key failure of the American national security system was the "failure of imagination." The dizzying array of technology that has emerged since the report, such as UAV's, virtual reality, AI, 3D Printing, and a panoply of other products, has exponentially increased the need for imagination.

The Dichotomy of Counterterrorism

There is a consistent dichotomy when considering the application of modern technological innovations in regards to terrorism. On one hand, there is an obvious and rational drive to develop novel advancements that can bring invaluable benefits for tracking malicious efforts. On the other hand, it is of great concern that chances for the malevolent exploitation of these forward-looking solutions increasingly exist. The difficulty for society to fully understand and integrate the range of emerging technologies has given rise to a common fallacy. There is an assumption that even though the general public struggles to make sense of the new technology violent non-state actors have the emergent threats themselves are not that significant. However, there is a correlation between rapid technological change and radical political action; the printing press helped accelerate the Protestant Reformation, the cassette tape and the direct dial telephone had a similar impact on the Iranian Revolution, and the rise of the internet fuelled the spread of both the Radical Right and Radical Islamists. This partial and reductionist view of complex historical forces, however, leads people to the conclusion that the radicals always win the technology battle. This is unlikely true as the process itself represents an offensive action and defensive reaction cycle.

Counterterrorism experts are required to keep pace with the incredible speed of modern technological innovations and to start thinking through the lens of high-tech evolutions for the following good reasons. Firstly, to better understand the current terrorist threat landscape, it is necessary to examine how these novelties have changed violent non-state actors' strategic and operational decision-making. It is also inevitable that one must recognise the impact of these developments in order to precisely assess the risks of terrorist activities. At the same time, the counterterrorism field itself must elaborate on ways in which these pioneering solutions can reduce their burdens. Instead of monitoring terrorists' high-tech practices only as reactive inspectors, scholars and practitioners can proactively apply modern technological innovations in measures designed to prevent or combat terrorism. To these ends, experts should engage in a widespread exchange of both case studies and best practices to effectively counter newly emerged terrorist tactics. In *Terrorism Futures: Evolving Technology and TTPs Use*, Bunker applies his years of experience in Future Studies, working with government and academia to bring a rigorous approach to understanding this crucial question.

The Future of Terrorism

The book is a compilation of nine essays Bunker produced for TRENDS Research and Analysis in Abu Dhabi, in which he addressed how technological trends intersect with and influence violent non-state actors and their Tactics, Targets and Procedures (TTPs). Each essay has a useful discussion on how the change in technology is also influencing the groups and the response communities' TTPs. The compilation of this series of essays informs the wider debate over aspects of the future of terrorism. The work avoids the usual hyperbole and offers a clear and well-informed view of the trends, and is a powerful endorsement of the value of properly conducted future studies. This work should assist in avoiding the past failure in imagination.

Bunker first examines how virtual reality and drones can change not only the nature of suicide terrorism, but also how it will impact the internal dynamics of those who choose traditional suicide operations with the new 'virtual martyrs'. His next two essays offer a valuable insight into how technology has broadened the ability of terrorists to attack not just the physical infrastructure of society, but the value of trust that enables all societies to function. Attacking the community bonds is significantly more disruptive to a society than any particular terrorist event. The key to this is the rapid ability to disseminate the event and message of the attack through social media. This is increasingly accomplished through bots and other tools artificially manipulating social media. This wider use of social media and other cyber tools has created a 5th dimension of warfare that that permits an actor to conduct wider asymmetric campaigns against a state. The range of cyber and information warfare tools can overwhelm militaries' and the wider societies' abilities to understand the nature of the conflict and take appropriate actions until it is too late. The fourth essay returns to the idea of suicide bombings but in a more conventional way. Bunker examines the shifting of both the nature of the explosives type and decreasing use of anti-personal shrapnel, as well as moving the location of the bombs, "close to the body," particularly the emerging trend of placing devices in underwear—as we in Sri Lanka know all too well—or inside the body. This changing nature of devices has implications for security response that Bunker also discusses.

The fifth section elaborates the applicability of LASER (Light Amplification by Stimulated Emission of Radiation) in the context of riots and terrorism. Over the last decade or more, international civil aviation has faced an increasing use of commercially available lasers targeting aircraft primarily on landing. There is little evidence of terrorist intent in these incidents, but the importance of raising the general issue of the use of lasers to the wider security community is a vital service. Drawing on the experienced merging of physical and cyber forms of terrorism, the discussion in the book continues with a separate section on trends in the manufacturing of homemade, printed, and teleoperated (remote) firearms. These novel tactical innovations combine various operational benefits. They offer the convenience of manufacturing the malicious device without any special laboratory circumstances while, on the top of that, perpetrators can enjoy the luxury of staying away from the scene.

The seventh essay investigates jihadist application of commercial bots and automated text systems. Having acknowledged the impact of online propaganda on future radicalization trends recommendations on the most effective countermeasures are put forward. The next section delivers a threat typology of vehicle borne improvised explosive devices (VBIEDs) together with a concise analysis on the associated terrorist potential. Simultaneously, particular attention has been given to the deployment of armoured VBIEDs in Iraq and Syria. The final, and ninth, essay examines and analyses the laptop bomb threat to civil aviation posed by radical Islamist groups using this novel IED form. It provides context related to past civil aviation bombings, the terrorism potentials stemming from this novel type of attack, and the resulting travel bans imposed on carry-on laptops and electronics by national governments as airliner security countermeasures.

This book is an excellent inventory of the most recent innovations in violent non-state actors' operational tactics, techniques, and procedures. I encourage all counter terrorism experts to study this material and get acquainted with the terrorist application of modern technological advancements in order to make better use of them. The credibility of the discussion in the book is further enhanced by the extensive expertise the author possesses. Besides being a highly-qualified trainer of counterterrorism practitioners, Bunker has been elaborating the theoretical perspectives of third generation technologies' impact on terrorism and insurgencies. He is one of the most productive scholars and practitioners engaging in analyses of emerging forms of conflict. He has also been investigating the potential changes in violent non-state actors' strategic and operational environment that technological innovations may induce. The scholarly and practitioner community is grateful to Bunker for pioneering and sustained contribution to understand and respond to future threats.

Dr. Rohan Gunaratna is Professor of Security Studies at Nanyang Technological University and Founder of the International Centre for Political Violence and Terrorism Research in Singapore. His many books include *Inside Al Qaeda: Global Network of Terror* (Columbia University Press, 2002).

Preface

Terrorism Futures

The *Terrorism Futures: Evolving Technology and TTPs Use* pocketbook is derived from a series of nine essays written by the author between December 2014 and June 2017 for TRENDS Research & Advisory, Abu Dhabi, United Arab Emirates. During this period, the author was a Non-Resident Counterterrorism Fellow with TRENDS and, in coordination with then Director of Research & Engagement, Dr. William Burchill, developed and contributed to its Terrorism Futures series while at the same time retaining copyright © to his intellectual products. With subsequent organizational and website changes at TRENDS and the departure of its initial President and Founder, Dr. Ahmed Al-Hamli, concern exists that these intellectual products will no longer be available to counterterrorism scholars and professionals for research purposes. Already, a majority of these essays are no longer accessible via the present iteration of the TRENDS Research & Advisory website as this independent and progressive think tank evolves and shifts its mission focuses over time.

In order to preserve this collection of forward-thinking counterterrorism writings, the author has elected to publish them as a **C/O Futures** pocketbook—both soft cover and electronically—in agreement with Xlibris publishers. The writings are reflective of the C/O Futures strategic consultancy mandate and focus which seeks to engage in socio-political and operational environment shaping and response. As we all realize, it is far better to be proactive rather than reactive in the formulation of our counterterrorism policies and measures and shape the operational environment (in essence, stack the deck) against those who seek to generate fear and terror directed at us and within our societies in the process of advancing their fringe political and socio-religious end states.

While most terrorist incidents are characterized by the use of the 'gun and the bomb,' these groups are expanding into both low- (e.g. knives and vehicular overruns) and high-end (e.g. weaponized drone and teleoperated static weapons platform) technology use and the TTPs supporting it. Further, novel variations on mid-range technology use—such as the armoring of VBIEDs (vehicle borne improvised explosive devices)—is also taking place along with the use of homemade or 3D (three dimensional) printed firearms. The author's expertise, spanning unconventional and advanced technology use by terrorist, insurgent, and other threat groupings, lends itself to such terrorism futures projections and assessments.

In addition to the core nine essays focusing upon evolving terrorist use of technology and TTPs (tactics, techniques, and procedures) the work also benefits from an acronyms listing, a foreword by respected international terrorism expert Dr. Rohan Gunaratna, a conclusion providing an overview of the technology and TTPs themes contained within the pocketbook—as well as candidate technologies and TTPs (e.g. first person shooter [FPS] and live streaming attacks) not initially discussed within the essays, along with a short section on further terrorism futures readings which may have some utility for the readers.

Essay 1

Virtual Martyrs—Jihadists, Oculus Rift, and IED Drones

For some decades now, jihadists (radical Islamists) have relied upon suicide bombings—primarily via individually carried and vehicular borne (VBIED) explosives—as a distinct form of terrorist attack. Individual martyrdom, as a blood sacrifice to god, is an integral component to many suicide bombings and utilized collectively for terrorist group cohesion and recruitment purposes in line with jihadist narratives and cult rhetoric. Of concern is the intersection of the two trends of virtual (augmented) reality and commercial drones (UAVs; unmanned aerial vehicles) utilized by terrorists which now offer the potential for a new variant of this form of terrorism to emerge—one based on the concept of the 'virtual martyr.' This short essay will express these concerns along with some of the implications of what this new type of 'bloodless martyrdom' may mean.

Virtual (Augmented) Reality

In an essay on the deeper implications of virtual reality (VR) on warfare, I recently summarized the emergence of VR as follows:

> Concepts of 'virtual reality,' an interactive artificial environment experienced by a human through computer generated sensory stimuli, have been around since the late 1950s/ early 1960s. Those concepts, along with the technology underlying them, have greatly evolved over the course of decades through flight simulators to various forms of scientific and entertainment visualization to augmented realities. Virtual reality, as an interactive human-computer experience, has utility in business, industry, science, entertainment and many other facets of early 21st century human civilization [1].

This form of technology has recently taken a great strive forward via the Oculus Rift system which offers an unparalleled 'wide field of view with head-tracking and stereoscopic 3D' for virtual world interaction and gaming [2]. One of the hurdles of creating this technology has been the 'motion sickness' effect of VR, which initially set this system back a number of years and was readily evident in the initial development kit [3].

Oculus Rift advantages include the fact that the headset, which covers the eyes and much of the face, is light weight (~13.4 oz) and comfortable to wear, has universal connectivity regarding cable interfaces and power sources, and even offers multiple eye cups for different vision needs. It is also readily affordable at $350.00 for the development kit 2 (pre-consumer release). With the backing of Facebook, which purchased Oculus Rift for $2 Billion back in July 2014 [4], the Beta market release of this product is currently set for the Summer of 2015 [5].

The military applications of this system are only beginning to be recognized and include Norwegian Army tank driving tests in May of 2014 which allowed the drivers to 'see through their vehicles' via 360-degree camera mounts while the external hatches are closed [6]. It was also reported that same month that the U.S. Defense Advanced Research Projects Agency (DARPA) may be creating virtual reality data coding interfaces which allow cyber soldiers to counter hacker intrusions launched against military networks [7].

Commercial Drones (UAVs) and Terrorism

Terrorists and insurgents, specifically radical Islamists but not just limited to such groups, have been considering the merits of taking commercial and gray-area (modified and with military components) drones and placing explosives on them for attack purposes since the early-to-mid 2000s. Other uses, such as for surveillance and as weapons platforms, have also been considered. About twenty terrorist and insurgent drone related incidents—procurement of components, seizure in raids, attempted use, and actual use—have now either taken place or been reported (but not fully confirmed).

Unmanned aerial vehicles in the possession of these groups, which now includes Al Qaeda (and affinity adherents), the Taliban, Islamic State, Hamas, and Hezbollah, have been documented in a growing list of media articles and think tank reports [8]. Al Qaeda affinity linked drone plots in the United States include the April 2007 Christopher Paul (Columbus, Ohio) [9] and September 2011 Rezwan Feradus (Ashland,

Massachusetts) incidents [10]. The latter incident is of note because the IED drones to be used—F-86 Sabre and F-4 Phantom scale model jets—also had GPS and high speed (+150 miles per hour) attributes giving them significant precision targeting and kinetic kill capabilities [11].

Such drone incidents have not subsided with three taking place in the last six months. A homemade Hamas drone, armed with what appears to be small rockets, was shot down in Ashdod, Israel in July 2014 [12], an Islamic State drone (a quadcopter) appears to have provided imagery of a Syrian army base prior to a ground assault in August 2014 [13], and Hezbollah released a video of what is said to be a drone attack on al-Nusra Front (Al Qaeda linked) personnel near Arsal, North East Lebanon [14].

Technology Fusion Potentials

It does not require much imagination to merge the trends of terrorist use of IED carrying drones (UAVs) with virtual reality technology such as Oculus Rift. In fact, a conceptual example already exists in the 'quadrotor racing' world, as can be viewed in a Youtube video from Argonay, France in September 2014 [15]. This video has already garnered over a million views so this event is now well known in the technorati circles.

In the video, about twenty drones and their operators, with immersion head gear, are involved in a forest race along a short course with drone speeds up to 50 kilometers (30 miles) per hour [16]. The placement of a small IED on these racing quads would be relatively easy for terrorist attack purposes and can be used for detonation against point (individual) and area (group) targets in the open or in confined areas (such as in a room with an open window) in an anti-personnel mode.

Dedicated IED drones can thus be created from the high-hundreds to low-thousands of dollars so that cost will not create a barrier to their use. Upgrades to such devices of course would include the Oculus Rift system, once it sees mass market release [17], and other technology enhancements such as GPS positioning and longer range C2 (command and control) links. Suffice it to say, the terrorist potentials of singular and multiple IED drone use are readily evident. Appropriate countermeasures and response protocols to this emergent threat, along with its being combined with a physical standup assault, now need to be at least considered and likely red teamed.

Virtual Martyr Implications

Beyond the practical terrorism threat, considerations of VR enabled IED drones will likely bring about a new concept— albeit gradually over time—which is that of the 'virtual martyr'. This form of radical Islamist martyr will differ greatly from that of its predecessor based on suicide bombing. Traditional terrorist martyrdom is derived from one's great commitment to the cause and the willingness to engage in self-sacrifice combined with relatively low technology applied in an in situ (non-stand-off) attack [18].

The virtual martyr, on the other hand, will be characterized as a technology savvy individual—yet one that is less willing to engage in the ultimate act of self-sacrifice. The attack itself will be dual-dimensional in nature, with the operator utilizing a virtual reality interface to remain in a stand-off mode while guiding the IED drone to its intended target. Whereas the traditional terrorist martyr has only one life to give in an attack, the virtual martyr— much like in a 3D action game—will have multiple lives to expend as long as additional IED drones exist for him or her to attack with.

Such Oculus Rift (and later generation VR interface) using terrorists will have become the virtual equivalent to the 'exploding man' [19] yet may likely be looked down upon by their more traditional brethren—at least at first. Whether the virtual martyr will be susceptible to PTSD (post-traumatic stress disorder) is unknown but this is just one of a number of questions this new concept may generate. The potentials of virtual martyrdom, however, do suggest that a second wave of 'suicide bombers' may indeed be released upon us sometime in the future—yet these VR based attackers will not die when their bombs explode as in the past. The practical TTP (tactics, techniques and procedures) and even ideological jihadist cohesion and radicalism implications of what this may mean, if it should come to pass, currently are unknown but are important factors to consider.

Notes

[1] Robert J. Bunker, "Is Virtual Reality Changing the Nature of War?" International Relations and Security Network (ISN). *ETH Zurich.* 20 June 2014, http://isn.ethz.ch/Digital-Library/Articles/Detail/?lng=en&id=180777.

[2] Oculus VR, LLC., "Oculus Rift: Next-Gen Virtual Reality," https://www.oculus.com/rift/.

[3] Kyle Orland, "Developer cites motion sickness in delaying Oculus Rift support." *Ars technica.* 21 August 2014, http://arstechnica.com/gaming/2014/08/developer-cites-motion-sickness-in-delaying-oculus-rift-support/.

[4] Stuart Dredge, "Facebook closes its $2bn Oculus Rift acquisition. What next?" *The Guardian.* 22 July 2014, http://www.theguardian.com/technology/2014/jul/22/facebook-oculus-rift-acquisition-virtual-reality.

[5] Hugh Langley, "The consumer-ready Oculus Rift will launch in public beta by summer 2015." *Techradar*. 11 September 2014, http://www.techradar.com/us/news/gaming/ the-consumer-ready-oculus-rift-will-launch-in-public-beta-by-summer-2015-1265010.

[6] Eirik Helland Urke, "Norwegian army driving armoured vehicle using Oculus Rift." TUTV. 5 May 2014, http://www.tu.no/ tutv/forsvar/2014/05/05/norwegian-army-driving-armoured-vehicle-using-oculus-rift and http://www.tujobs.com/news/ 238400-see-the-norwegian-armed-forces-driving-with-oculus-rift.

[7] Joseph Mayton, "DARPA uses Oculus Rift technology to prep military for cyberwarfare." *Tech Times*. 27 May 2014, http://www.techtimes.com/articles/7512/20140527/darpa-uses-oculus-rift-technology-to-prep-military-for-cyber-warfare.htm.

[8] For an early work, see Eugene Miasnikov, Threat of Terrorism Using Unmanned Aerial Vehicles: Technical Aspects. Moscow: Center for Arms Control, Energy and Environmental Studies at MIPT, June 2004. Translated in English—March 2005, http:// www.armscontrol.ru/uav/report.htm.

[9] Bob Driehaus, "U.S. Indicts an Ohio Man in Terror Conspiracy Case." *The New York Times*. 13 April 2007, http:// www.nytimes.com/2007/04/13/us/13ohio.html?fta=y&_r=0.

[10] Peter Finn, "Mass. man accused of plotting to hit Pentagon and Capitol with drone aircraft." *The Washington Post*. 28 September 2011, http://www.washingtonpost.com/ national/national-security/mass-man-accused-of-plotting-

to-hit-pentagon-and-capitol-with-drone-aircraft/2011/09/28/
gIQAWdpk5K_story.html.

[11] For the speed and other specifications of the F-86 Sabre
model, see http://www.jethangar.com/Aircraft/Sabre/F86.html.

[12] Isabel Kershner and Patrick J. Lyons, "Hamas Publishes
Photo of a Drone It Says It Built." *The New York Times*. 14 July
2014, http://www.nytimes.com/2014/07/15/world/middleeast/
hamas-publishes-photo-of-a-drone-it-says-it-built.html.

[13] Yasmin Tadjdeh, "Islamic State Militants in Syria Now
Have Drone Capabilities." *National Defense Magazine*. 28
August 2014, http://www.nationaldefensemagazine.org/blog/
Lists/Posts/Post.aspx?ID=1586.

[14] Peter Bergen and Emily Schneider, "Hezbollah
armed drone? Militants' new weapon." *CNN News*. 22
September 2014, http://www.cnn.com/2014/09/22/opinion/
bergen-schneider-armed-drone-hezbollah/.

[15] Herve Pellarin, "Drone racing star wars style Pod racing
are back!" YouTube. 30 September 2014, https://www.youtube.
com/watch?v=ZwL0t5kPf6E.

[16] Elliot Williams, "Quadrotor Pod Racing." *Hackaday*.
6 October 2014, http://hackaday.com/2014/10/06/
quadrotor-pod-racing/.

[17] Oculus Rift has already been interfaced with drone
controllers. See, for example, Karissa Bell, "Parrot Introduces
Oculus Rift-Enabled Drone." *Mashable*. 11 May 2014,
http://mashable.com/2014/05/11/parrot-bebop-drone/, and

ARDroneShow.com, "Flying Parrot Bebop Drone with Sky Controller & Oculus Rift." YouTube. 12 May 2014, https://www.youtube.com/watch?v=HmoD0HVOVcI.

[18] This description represents the traditional martyrdom archetype. Numerous examples of coercion, family payment, mental instability, and drugging suicide bombers exist which means this archetype cannot be universally applied.

[19] See Christopher Flaherty, "Chapter 5: Victim, Martyr, or Retaliation, and Becoming the Bomb." In Robert J. Bunker and Christopher Flaherty, *Body Cavity Bombers: The New Martyrs—A Terrorism Research Center Book*. Bloomington: iUniverse, 2013: 170-172.

Further Readings

Robert J. Bunker, "Is Virtual Reality Changing the Nature of War?" International Relations and Security Network (ISN). *ETH Zurich*. 20 June 2014, http://isn.ethz.ch/Digital-Library/Articles/Detail/?lng=en&id=180777.

Robert J. Bunker, *Terrorist and Insurgent Unmanned Aerial Vehicles: Use, Potentials, and Military Implications*. Carlisle, PA: Strategic Studies Institute, US Army War College, August 2015: 1-70, https://press.armywarcollege.edu/monographs/445/.

Bryan Harris, "Emerging technologies to turn suicide bombers into 'virtual martyrs', experts predict." *South China Morning Post*. 18 January 2015, https://www.scmp.com/news/world/article/1681606/emerging-technologies-turn-suicide-bombers-virtual-martyrs-experts.

Essay 2

Terrorism as Disruptive Targeting

This short Terrorism Futures essay will focus upon differing forms of targeting and their effects, that is, destructive versus disruptive, and the interrelationship between these and the scale of effect of weaponry in engagements, highlighting the differences between legitimate state use of coercion and the illegitimate use of disruptive targeting—and the subsequent magnification of the scale of effect of weaponry in engagements—when employed by terrorists. It will conclude with a discussion of the counter-threat implications of acknowledging terrorism as a form of disruptive targeting and the need for states to focus on new counter-threat protocols that go beyond physical consequence management and instead also include the protection of societal bonds.

Terrorism Versus State Coercion

States as legitimate sovereigns seek to utilize coercion via the certainty of punishment by means of fines, incarceration, and—in certain circumstances—capital punishment to enforce societal norms and rules to both protect and benefit its citizens and foreign nationals residing within its borders. The end result sought is one in which the integrity of society is maintained for the public good and the bonds and relations between the governed and the government remain positive and strong. Acknowledged tradeoffs between personal freedoms and security are an accepted component of the metrics related to a state's use of internal coercion directed against its citizenry. Failure to maintain balance—derived from historical norms of expected governance—may result in civil protest and unrest, especially if perceptual gaps exists such as between a minority of the populace and larger components of society. This issue has recently come to the fore with race and justice issues in the United States related to the Ferguson incident [1].

A legitimate state's concerns over internal stability can be strongly contrasted to the use of terrorism by a non-state group acting independently or as a proxy for a foreign state [2]. Since the intent of terrorism is to degrade the internal stability of a state in order to achieve concessions and/or change governance to further its own group's (or sponsor's) policies, it is used to de-bond societal cohesion rather than reinforce it. The certainty of the use of coercion is thus of no utility to the terrorist who comes from a position antithetical to that of the state. Thus, an ambiguity in approach (or at least the perception of one) is strived for because it generates more apprehension within targeted populations due to the uncertainty if or when an attack may come and magnifies the resulting disruptive effects.

Destructive Versus Disruptive Targeting

When sovereign states—which are hierarchically based—undertake conventional warfare with one another, the natural form of combat targeting is destructive in nature. It is directed at 'things' such as people (the citizenry), the government, and the military of opposing states. Destructive targeting is thus very thing based—be it measured in ground seized, people captured or killed, or materiel destroyed.

A second form of targeting—known as disruptive targeting—has more recently been identified over the last few decades. This form of targeting is organic to more networked organizational forms such as non-state groups. Since evolved networks are, by their nature, redundant in information flows and have a capacity to self-heal by working around damaged nodes [3], they utilize disruptive means for conflict (fighting) purposes. Instead of targeting 'things' (such as people or nodes), the target sets attacked are the 'bonds and relationships' that connect things together [4]. Trust between citizens, civilian feelings of security within a society, and goodwill between the people and their government are but a few examples of such target sets.

Conventional military operations related to such targeting draw upon principles of psychological warfare and getting inside an opposing force's OODA (observe-orient-decide-act) loop. Concepts of blitzkrieg (maneuver warfare) in which the actions of an attacking army causes cascading command and control (C2) failure and eventual paralysis within an opposing armed force also succeed by getting into this loop. The disruptive nature of this form of military targeting, however, is not generally emphasized given that it is still directed toward a parallel conventional force. Terrorism, by creating a climate of terror within the targeted population and thereby breaking the bonds of security and trust within society, on the other hand, represents a clearer form of disruptive targeting—one which is criminal (illegal) in nature and condemned for breaking the rules and conduct of civilized warfare and internationally agreed upon norms and laws.

Point, Area, and Systemic Effects

The scale of effect of weaponry in military and military-like engagements takes place at ever increasing levels of battlespace influence (e.g. operational space for policing). At the most basic level, point targets—that is individuals—engage utilizing bladed weapons and small arms. The next level of effect encompasses an area, essentially a cluster of points, which may include shooting at a line of individual targets or throwing a grenade into a grouping of targets.

The final level of effect is systemic in nature with the result that large clusters of individuals (or nodes) are being influenced by the attack or engagement. Large scale physical systemic effects are difficult to create with conventional (explosive based weapons and munitions) and bring us into the realm of CBRN (chemical, biological, radiological, and nuclear) [5] and information/cyber based attacks (drawing upon computer viruses and radio frequency (RFW)/high-power microwave (HPM) type weaponry) [6].

The scale of the effect of different weaponry and engagement patterns, however, combine with the type of effect of differential forms of targeting resulting in dissimilar end states for coercion and terrorism. With regard to the scale and type of effect, Figure 1. is illustrative of the difference between a tactical action (point—or even area—focused based on destructive targeting) and a terrorist event (systemic focused based on disruptive targeting) [7].

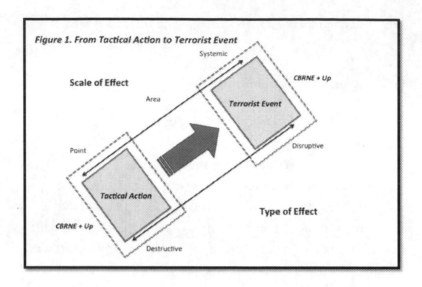

Figure 1. From Tactical Action to Terrorist Event

A terrorist attack, on its own, is basically meaningless when viewed from a conventional warfare perspective—it is typically equivalent to, at best, a squad sized force engagement. However, because such an attack is not about destructive potentials but rather focused on disruptive ones, it can readily result in systemic (strategic) level influence outcomes. One can think of the attack as dropping a pebble into a tranquil pond—the point of impact is inconsequential—rather the ripples created on the pond surface serves as the attacking mechanism [8].

Unlike when a conventional force engages in an action, a terrorist event results in a synergistic outcome. A tactical action by conventional forces targeting one individual or a group of individuals will result in physical damage to only the same number of those engaged. A terrorist event, however, may result in the death of a limited number of people but, because of its disruptive effects, 'terrorizes' at a systemic level all of those individuals who identify at some level with its victim(s). While the mechanism involved may be inherently irrational in nature, the attack plays on the fears of a state's citizens and the disruptive effects of the attack are reinforced by the sensationalized and repetitive nature of 21st century global media.

Counter-Threat Implications

In line with the previous discussion, and as can be seen in Figure 2., the difference in the purpose of a state's use of coercion (to—along with inducements—reinforce societal cohesion) versus that of non-state independent and state-proxy terrorism (to de-bond social cohesion) come into the equation. This terrorist *offensive* versus sovereign state *defensive* dynamic means that counter-terrorism response cannot be focused solely on threat force tactical actions and their destructive effects [9]. Too often, consequence management is 'thing' focused—the natural bias of states—with effort simply put into the treatment of those injured in an attack and the physical clean-up of incident scenes with lip service given to alleviate public fears. Given the Westphalian origins of modern states, protecting the integrity of the links between their government, people, and military sectors is paramount.

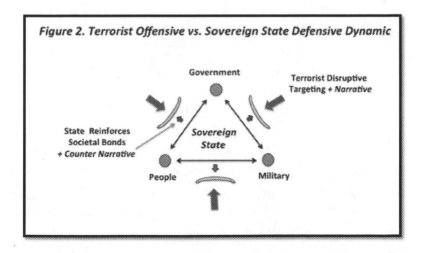

Figure 2. Terrorist Offensive vs. Sovereign State Defensive Dynamic

Hence, a state must also fully engage in non-physical consequence management—writ large—in response to a terrorist attack. This form of response is needed to both counter the 'terrorist narrative' (i.e. the policies and end states that they are promoting) that is a component of an attack and, potentially even more importantly, to make sure societal bonds and relationships (i.e. citizen's trust in government, their feelings of security to engage in normal activities, and their sense of goodwill towards the military and law enforcement) have not been degraded or even potentially severed.

Given that advances in social media and global communications have moved us beyond 24/7 news channel platforms into torrents of live streaming information utilizing chats, tweets, and posts with embedded videos (some in real time), the disruptive potentials of terrorism will continually expand. It is imperative that sovereign states recognize such potentials by fully acknowledging the disruptive targeting basis from which terrorism is derived. In order to do so, they should now focus on implementing counter-threat protocols focusing on protecting and making resilient our vital societal bonds.

Notes

[1] Eliott C. McLaughlin, "What we know about Michael Brown's shooting." *CNN*. 15 August 2014, http://www.cnn.com/2014/08/11/us/missouri-ferguson-michael-brown-what-we-know/.

[2] Recent scholarship has attempted to shift traditional perceptions of terrorism from non-state groups (and, in some instances, their state sponsors) to now encompass specific internal policies and activities of states themselves. These perceptions fail to appreciate important categorical differences.

For a work showing a possible exception with regard to a fully illegitimate regime, see Paul Rexton Kan, Bruce E. Bechtol Jr., and Robert M. Collins, *Criminal Sovereignty: Understanding North Korea's Illicit International Activities*. Carlisle: Strategic Studies Institute, U.S. Army War College, 12 April 2010, http://www.strategicstudiesinstitute.army.mil/pubs/display.cfm?pubID=975.

[3] A basic primer on the differences between hierarchical and networked organizational forms is Ori Brafman and Rod A. Beckstrom, *The Starfish and the Spider: The Unstoppable Power of Leaderless Organizations*. New York: Portfolio, 2006.

[4] In addition to the author's bond-relationship targeting (BRT) research, the older netwar writings of John Arquilla and David Ronfeldt associated with the U.S. Naval Post Graduate School and RAND, respectively, should be consulted. See, for example, their *Advent of Netwar* (RAND 1996) and *Networks and Netwars* (RAND 2001).

[5] This is typically designated as CBRNE with the E representing 'explosives' that fall under very broad U.S. Federal "weapons of mass destruction" criteria for prosecution and sentencing purposes. Explosives, however, do not organically have a systemic level scale of effect—still, the E is considered part of the '+ Up' for destructive and disruptive effects.

[6] For some early thinking on these systemic effects, see Robert J. Bunker, "Weapons of Mass Disruption and Terrorism." *Terrorism and Political Violence*. Vol. 12. No. 1. Spring 2000: 37-46.

[7] This figure is modified from Figure 7: BCB Scale of Effect and Type of Effect found in Robert J. Bunker and Christopher Flaherty, *Body Cavity Bombers: The New Martyrs—A Terrorism Research Center Book*. Bloomington: iUniverse, 2013: 245.

[8] Using this analogy, CBRNE, with E dependent on use—as 9/11 utilized this form of weaponry (kinetic force and fuel loads of jet liners), can be viewed as dropping a rock into a pond rather than a pebble in that the disruptive surface ripples will be far larger.

[9] Components of this response, of course, include terrorist recruitment, funding, and other counter-organizational element focuses meant to deter, degrade, and ultimately eliminate terrorist groups operating locally and internationally via cooperation with partner nations.

Further Readings

Robert J. Bunker, "Weapons of Mass Disruption and Terrorism." *Terrorism and Political Violence*. Vol. 12. No. 1. Spring 2000: 37-46.

Robert J. Bunker, "Bond-Relationship Targeting." *Leatherneck*. 22 March 2006, http://www.leatherneck.com/forums/showthread.php?27811-Bond-Relationship-Targeting.

Robert J. Bunker, "Battlespace Dynamics, Information Warfare to Netwar, and Bond-Relationship Targeting." *Small Wars & Insurgencies*. Vol. 13, Iss. 2, 2008: 97-108.

Essay 3

Fifth Dimensional Battlespace—
Terrorism and Counter-
Terrorism Implications

This essay in the Terrorism Futures series will highlight the emergence of fifth dimensional battlespace, its implications for both the conduct of terrorism and counterterrorism operations, and, to some extent, interactions with terrorist disruptive targeting capabilities. Additionally, the larger civilizational context in which a dynamic yet little recognized terrorism and counterterrorism 'fifth dimensional capabilities race' that is taking place will be highlighted. While initially this concept may seem abstract, the importance of understanding its implications will become apparent.

Fifth Dimensional Battlespace

The concept of fifth dimensional battlespace is derived from the recognition of the growing influence of cyber (informational) and hyper (geometric) dimensionality on conflict and war. An early writer on the cyber component of this new form of space was William Gibson. He wrote the celebrated 1980s cyberpunk novel *Neuromancer* in which he defined cyberspace as:

> A consensual hallucination experienced daily by billions of legitimate operators, in every nation, by children being taught mathematical concepts... A graphic representation of data abstracted from banks of every computer in the human system. Unthinkable complexity. Lines of light ranged in the nonspace of the mind, clusters and constellations of data. Like city lights, receding...[1].

Even earlier geometric artistic genres focusing on tesseracts and hypercubes—such as the Crucifixion (Corpus Hypercubus) by Salvador Dali in 1954—are also reflective of this emerging form of space-time interaction [2].

This form of advanced dimensionality—what was once only considered as relevant to 20th century art and science fiction—has in the 21st century been increasingly identified for its military and law enforcement applicability. The essential lesson learned is that human state forms and society build upon environmental and technological foundations as the energy basis of civilization (e.g. derived from human, animal, machine forms) has evolved over the course of many centuries. Along with this evolutionary process comes mastery of space-time dimensionality within increasing advanced forms of battlespace itself—whether it be the two dimensional battlespace of the ancients (x; line space + t; time) or the three dimensional battlespace of the medieval world (x,y; plane space + t; time). Thus, the battlespace—where humans fight and die—of antiquity or even the middle ages is fundamentally different in its level of sophistication (as are the armaments, armor, and even mounts utilized) compared to that which is presently utilized in our modern four dimensional world (See Fig. 1).

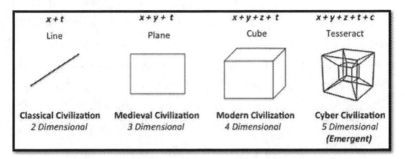

Source: *Fifth Dimensional Operations: Space-Time-Cyber Dimensionality in Conflict and War—A Terrorism Research Center Book:* 184.

Four dimensional battlespace, which is essentially composed of a maneuver and targeting box that is iterated in nature (x,y,z; cube space + t; time), has for roughly five-hundred years been the dominant physical area in which military forces have engaged one another. This form of battlespace, which the U.S. and coalition forces proved to have complete mastery of in the two Iraq Wars against Saddam Hussein (identifying and precision targeting his opposing military forces at will), however, is now beginning to near the end of its functional utility due to the advent of a more advanced form of battlespace derived from fifth dimensional attributes.

This form of emergent battlespace, which contains cyber (c) and hyper (h) elements of dimensionality, allows for the application of new informational and geometric based capabilities in conflict and war. One component of this advanced form of battlespace is the existence of a "human sensing dimensional barrier" that separates cyberspace (the fifth dimension) from humanspace (four dimensional space) even though they simultaneously exist together within the same physical area [3]. Another component of this form of battlespace is that of a force now able to engage in military activities that could not be conducted before due to restrictions imposed by earlier space-time barriers. With these barriers now overcome, qualitatively new warfighting capabilities are gained. As more and more components of fifth dimensional battlespace emerge, both terrorists and responding security forces will utilize them just as the military forces of more technologically advanced states are beginning to do [4].

Terrorism Implications

A five dimensional space analysis of defensive and offensive terrorist TTPs (tactics, techniques, and procedures) yields new insights into how these violent non-state actors engage in their operations. Terrorist use the defensive benefits of 'cyberspace' via stealth masking to dimensionally shift out of the killing ground of humanspace (e.g. four dimensional space). If it were not for this stealth masking capability, such forces would be easily acquired by security forces and either arrested or killed once inside sovereign state territories. Terrorist gain this dimensional shifting capability by means of a simple cost-effective cheat— they do not wear national military uniforms that identify them as enemy combatants. For advanced nation state forces—that follow the rules of warfare—to obtain a similar capability, they must field advanced (and costly) sensor defeating forces such as stealth aircraft that eliminate radar cross section (RCS), thermal emissions, and other signatures of their existence in physical space. In both instances—be it a terrorist or advanced stealth platform, they can be viewed as an invisible force that has defensively shifted (via spatial expansion—moving two points in space and time away from other) out of the killing zone of modern battlespace.

The offensive benefits of cyberspace provide terrorists with the ability to reach beyond the battlefield in which a tactical action takes place and influence civilian populations that are far away from the incident for psychological warfare (terroristic) purposes. The United States first truly encountered this phenomenon during the Vietnam War (a television war) and was finally defeated in that conflict due to the 1968 Tet Offensive which, while a physical victory for the U.S., lost that nation the war due to the final severing of its domestic bonds and relationships derived from disruptive targeting effects [5]. The term for the fifth dimensional capability that allowed the terrorizing of U.S. civilian populations which ultimately influenced the outcome of that war is known as spatial contraction [6]—the ability to take two points in time and space and bring them together (e.g. in this instance, civilians via media links to the battlefield). Over the course of decades, taped media shown during the evening news hour (which was delayed in its viewing) has been replaced with 24 hour news channels (that are more timely in their event broadcasting) and, ultimately, real time feeds and links by means of webcams, Skype, Tweets, and other social media technologies that have greatly increased offensive terrorist disruptive capabilities via this process of spatial contraction.

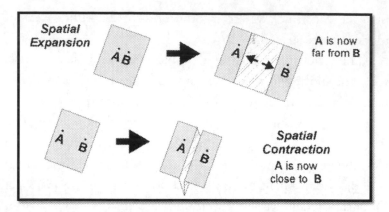

Source: *Five-Dimensional (Cyber) Warfighting*: 9.

Counter-Terrorism Implications

While the emergence of fifth dimensional space has provided both defensive and offensive capabilities to terrorists, it also has provided new capabilities to state security forces. As a result, a little noticed 'fifth dimensional capabilities race' has been taking place between terrorists and insurgents that wish to attack sovereign states and the public agents (police, security, and military personnel) that seek to defend them. One readily identifiable capability that is increasingly being utilized by state forces is the use of data fusion systems which attempt to identify stealth masked terrorists and bring them out of the defensive bastion of cyberspace into the killing (or capturing) ground of humanspace.

This is accomplished by piercing the "human sensing dimensional barrier" that stealth masked forces utilize thus allowing for them to then be acquired in time and space. Facial recognition and (less mature) 'hostile intent' technologies represent two examples of this process. They can be deployed at entry chokepoints, such as international airports, and are used to scan for terrorists attempting to enter national borders [7].

New body scanning machines—based on millimeter wave technology—in airports also fall into this countermeasure capability by looking for weapons hidden under clothing as do radar systems used by SWAT (special weapons and tactics) teams that can see movement and other activity (through physical walls) taking place inside terrorist hostage barricade situations.

New advanced weaponry capabilities—based on directed energy systems—that overcome prior space-time limitations (such as ballistics) are also emerging that state security forces can utilize against terrorist forces. These systems, such as the Active Denial System (ADS), allow for the generation of pain-inducing 'energy barriers' in physical space as well as the potential ability to counter terrorist human shield scenarios by incapacitating individuals (both the terrorist and the hostages/confederates) rather than utilizing deadly force [8]. The creation of 'optical walls' (laser based) to visually inhibit would-be suicide bombers from approaching security check points and 'energy shields' projected over facilities that pre-detonate mortar rounds fired by terrorist operatives readily provide additional examples of such capabilities [9].

Broader Context of Evolving Dimensionality and Change

Ultimately, the emergence of fifth dimensional battlespace as the new high ground (dimensionally speaking) in war and conflict, is representative of a shift from the modern (Westphalian state system) to the post-modern (successor and challenger state forms) era in human civilization. This shift is already underway in advanced economies with the fielding of 3D (three dimensional), and even newer 4D (four dimensional; self-assembly over time) [10], printing systems that are now beginning to both revolutionize post-industrial production processes as well as influence military logistics [11]. It is imperative within the context of these and other great scientific changes now taking place in our world—such as in the fields of bio- and nano-technology—that sovereign state forces learn how to achieve mastery of the capabilities offered by the post-modern battlespace. This must be accomplished, while at the same time, denying such mastery to terrorist forces that are readily seeking to do harm to sovereign states and their peoples.

Notes

[1] William Gibson, *Neuromancer*. New York: Ace Books, 1984: 51. This early definition of cyberspace has been linked to concepts of virtual reality, however, fifth dimensional space is far more encompassing than just an interactive artificial environment utilized by human beings.

[2] For an image of this work, see "The Collection Online: Crucifixion (Corpus Hypercubus)." The Metropolitan Museum of Art, http://www.metmuseum.org/collection/the-collection-online/search/488880.

[3] The military basis of this conceptualization of dual-dimensional battlespace was developed in Robert J. Bunker, "Advanced Battlespace and Cybermaneuver Concepts: Implications for Force XXI." *Parameters*. Autumn 1996: 108-120, http://strategicstudiesinstitute.army.mil/pubs/parameters/Articles/96autumn/bunker.htm.

[4] For an overview and newer works on this advanced form of battlespace, see Robert J. Bunker and Charles "Sid" Heal, Editors, *Fifth Dimensional Operations: Space-Time-Cyber*

Dimensionality in Conflict and War—A Terrorism Research Center Book. Bloomington: iUniverse, 2014.

[5] Hence, terrorist disruptive targeting and fifth dimensional capabilities are intimately linked together, see Robert J. Bunker, "Terrorism as Disruptive Targeting." *TRENDS Research & Advisory.* January 2015, http://trendsinstitution.org/?p=870.

[6] On the flip side, the stealth masking (or dimensionally shifting) of forces can be viewed as spatial expansion. Two points in time and space that may be a few feet from one another, such as a terrorist standing in front of a state security officer, can for all intents and purposes be considered thousands of miles apart because the security officer cannot identify the terrorist as a threat but rather sees them as a random civilian (non-combatant).

[7] This, of course, means that state security forces know what the face of the terrorist entering into the nation looks like.

[8] For a primer on the ADS see U.S. Department of Defense, "Active Denial System FAQs." *Joint Non-Lethal Weapons Program,* nd, http://jnlwp.defense.gov/About/FrequentlyAskedQuestions/ActiveDenialSystemFAQs.aspx.

[9] The 'optical wall' capability is attributed to the Laser Dazzler while the 'energy dome' capability is attributed to the Shortstop system.

[10] For more on 4D printing, see Skylar Tibbits, "The emergence of '4D printing.'" *TED Talks.* February 2013, http://www.ted.com/talks/skylar_tibbits_the_emergence_of_4d_printing?language=en.

[11] For military logistics concerning 3D spare parts fabrication, see Sydney J. Freeberg, Jr., "Navy Warship is Taking Printing to Sea; Don't Expect a Revolution." *Breaking Defense.* 22 April 2014, http://breakingdefense.com/2014/04/navy-carrier-is-taking-3d-printer-to-sea-dont-expect-a-revolution/, Adam Asclipiadis, "Rapid Equipping Force uses 3-D printing on the frontline." *U.S. Army.* 9 July 2014, http://www.army.mil/article/129635/Rapid_Equipping_Force_uses_3_D_printing_on_the_frontline/, and Sarah Anderson, "China's PLA Navy Deploys 3D Printers Onboard Warships to Replace Small Parts." *3D Print.* 8 January 2015, http://3dprint.com/35981/china-pla-navy-3d-printing/.

Further Readings

Robert J. Bunker, "Advanced Battlespace and Cybermaneuver Concepts: Implications for Force XXI." *Parameters.* Autumn 1996: 108-120, https://press.armywarcollege.edu/parameters/vol26/iss3/4/.

Robert J. Bunker, *Five-Dimensional (Cyber) Warfighting.* Carlisle, PA: Strategic Studies Institute, US Army War College (1998): 1-42, https://press.armywarcollege.edu/monographs/171/.

Robert J. Bunker and Charles "Sid" Heal, Editors, *Fifth Dimensional Operations: Space-Time-Cyber Dimensionality in Conflict and War—A Terrorism Research Center Book.* Bloomington: iUniverse, 2014: 1-290.

Essay 4

Close to the Body and Body Cavity Suicide Bombs

The variation in human borne suicide bomb types used by terrorist organizations is much broader than is typically realized due to a number of iterations that have taken place over the course of decades. In this installment of the Terrorism Futures series, the more specialized close to the body and body cavity types will be focused upon. In addition, HAZMAT (hazardous materials) variants will be discussed along with the future potentials of these devices and the increased security interest in detecting them.

Suicide Bomb Iterations

Suicide bomb use can be traced back to at least the late 19th century and has had relatively high frequency of use since the early 1980s:

> Literally thousands of suicide bombings have taken place since Polish anarchist Ignacy

Hryniewiecki assassinated Czar Alexander II of Russia in 1881 by throwing a bomb at the Czar (Hryniewiecki died from wounds suffered from the resulting blast). Modern suicide bombings, however, have their historical origins in military force-on-force actions that then saw irregular forces and urban guerrillas transition into modern terrorists utilizing such devices [1].

While not specifically involving a 'suicide bomb', the known frequency of deaths to anarchists from such actions would mean that the bomber recognized it as a likely 'suicide mission'. World War II and Vietnam War era suicide bomb use for force-on-force engagements transitioned into Hizbollah suicide attacks on Israeli Defense Forces in southern Lebanon. These, in turn, gave way to suicide attacks by various terrorist organizations against civilians and other non-military targets. During this period, a transition from destructive to disruptive targeting took place. As a result, the explosive devices utilized were no longer necessarily military grade. Improvised equipment thus took precedence due to both the inability to acquire military munitions and the increasing need for creative ways to bypass security in order to deliver bombs to their targets [2].

A specialized variation of such terrorist devices are those meant to be much harder to detect than a traditional suicide bomb such as a military grade explosive satchel. These stealthy devices are utilized against hard targets (i.e. those with high levels of security projecting them) as opposed to conventional explosive devices utilized against soft targets (i.e. undefended ones). The trade off with such specialized devices is one between increased non-detectability and decreased functionality.

Low-to-no metal content as well as limiting the release of explosive trace vapors (or using less favored chemical compounds not normally searched for) and relying upon creative detonation protocols is strived for in these bombs to elude typical screening measures. Due to these bomb masking approaches, these types of explosive devices are more prone to either malfunction and lack of detonation or even pre-detonation such as in the case of TATP (triacetone triperoxide) based bombs [3]. Lethality levels of these explosive devices, however, also generally dropped as less metal content (lack of rigid containment) resulted in less pressure build up and fragmentation effects.

Close to the Body Suicide Bombs

For some decades now, overt suicide satchels, vests, and belts have been replaced in terrorist attacks on more heavily guarded venues, gatherings, and individuals by close to the body bombs—that is, bombs under the clothing of the perpetrator and/or close to their skin [4]. The intent is to mask the presence of the explosive devices from the view of security forces—be they law enforcement, military, state agents, or private contractor.

Such close to the body explosive device incidents readily number in the dozens and have resulted in the death and injury of hundreds of, if not well over a thousand, civilians and state security personnel. The attackers have utilized both traditional garments—such as turbans, robes, and burqas—under which bombs have been hidden as well as Western dress such as large jackets and loose fitting pants with devices strapped to the thighs or ankles. Women have also been made to feign pregnancy (utilized more than once by the Kurdish PKK) with a large explosive payload subsequently detonated.

Knowing that security pat-downs may detect these devices prior to attacking certain targets, terrorist groups have decided to get even more intimate and creative in their hiding of these bombs. As a result, bombs hidden under female breasts and in the genital areas of men and women have been utilized as well as bombs placed inside shoes or in the linings of jackets.

Well known incidents of close to the body bomb use are the December 2001 Richard Reid attempted shoe bomb detonation on American Airlines Flight 63 and the December 2009 Umar Farouk Abdulmutallab attempted underwear bomb detonation on Northwest Flight 253. Not all such attempts have been failures. What is generally forgotten is that such attacks—a case in point is the August 2004 Chechen 'black widow' bombers utilizing bra and/or waist bombs—were successful in bringing down two Russian commercial airliners ninety minutes apart and killing about ninety people. Subsequently, in September 2004, as an outcome of these attacks the US TSA (Transportation Security Administration) made changes to their pat-down policies [5].

Body Cavity Suicide Bombs

For extremely high value targets—such as commercial airliners and state officials—increased security protocols (e.g. body scans that peer under clothing and examine shoes and liquids for hidden explosives) have resulted in the shift away from close to the body bombs and the initial fielding of body cavity bombs. These devices are even harder to detect than bombs hidden next to the body but, as a result, suffer even more from decreased functionality and lethality [6].

Projected use concerns over such devices date to at least late 2006 with the Fadhel al-Maliki incident taking place in March 2007 at Los Angeles International Airport (LAX) seen as a classic I&W (indications & warnings) event. Airport travelers do not normally carry wires, a magnet (or rock), and a putty-like substance in their rectums along with manifesting lots of other suspicious behaviors all at once—carrying lots of $100 bills and being unable to account for recent activities for instance.

The first use of a body cavity bomb subsequently took place in Saudi Arabia with the assassination attempt on Saudi Prince Mohammed bin Nayef in August 2009 by Al Qaeda operative Abdullah al-Asiri. This was followed by another incident in December 2012 in which a Taliban agent attempted to kill Asadullah Khalid, head of Afghanistan's National Directorate of Security, with another rectum bomb. While bin Nayef escaped with only minor injuries, Khalid suffered severe injuries [7]. These injuries could have been worse if it were not for the fact that design limitations of these devices and the water content within the bomber's body itself dissipates much of the blast effects.

Biological, Chemical, and Radiological Variants

HAZMAT dispersal options with these types of explosive devices are chemical, biological and radiological (CBR) in nature. Essentially, a small explosive charge serves to scatter a hazardous substance for antipersonnel or area denial purposes. Chemical agents can range from simple riot control agents through industrial chemicals such as chlorine and phosgene into dedicated nerve agents such as sarin and the various V-series products. Biological substances may include ricin (a toxin), anthrax, HIV, ebola, or pathogens. Radiological elements (e.g. plutonium, uranium et al.) may include low-level radioactive hospital and fuel wastes along with more dangerous intermediate fuels and high-level fuel and weapons grade materials.

The positive news, however, is attempts to blend HAZMAT materials with close to the body and body cavity suicide bombs has been infrequent at best. At least one hepatitis infected suicide bomber was utilized by Palestinian extremists as well as fragmentation being laced with rat poison (an anti-coagulant) some years ago but both plots proved relatively ineffective—further, the suicide bombs carried were more conventional in nature [8]. Also, since chemical and biological agent effectiveness may be degraded by device detonation, terrorists do not tend to favor this dispersal method. While a radiological device might offer more effectiveness, both the potential metal content of the material itself and its radioactive nature would likely trigger screening sensors protecting more secure targets.

Future Potentials

Presently, close to the body and internal body explosive devices utilized by suicide bombers appear on a linear trajectory of design and employment with very limited interest in utilizing them as HAZMAT dispersal devices. Non-detectability of these devices will be stressed over functionality. Disruptive effects—the 'generation of terror'—will also continue to be stressed over destructive targeting. However, the basic assassination potentials of these devices should not be overlooked. It should be remembered that Rajiv Gandhi, former Prime Minister of India, was killed by a close to the body device carried by a female LTTE operative in May 1991 and Hashmat Khalil Karzai, a cousin of the Afghani president, was killed in July 2014 during a ritual greeting with a 16 year old bomber that detonated an explosive device hidden in his turban [9].

Advances in nano-explosives represent a wild card in regard to the increased future effectiveness of these devices. Some professionals have discounted the impact such technology may offer while others project future lethality increases [10]. One variant on internal bombs—utilizing basic liquid flammables internally carried to generate arson attacks on commercial aircraft—must also be considered as a potentially dangerous terrorist TTP (tactics, techniques, and procedures) that could emerge.

While close to the body and internal body suicide bombs represent a small percentage of overall suicide bombs that have been deployed, the fact that they are meant to be utilized against hard targets and hence high value in nature makes detecting them of great importance. This has resulted in new forms of screening technologies being developed and even dedicated forums being created so that the heightened threat they represent can be actively discussed by security professionals [11].

Notes

[1] Robert J. Bunker, "The Evolution of Terrorist Bombings." *Front Line Defence*. Vol. 11., No. 4. 2014, http://www.frontline-defence.com/index_archives.php?page=2207.

[2] Ibid; for a more in depth overview of these stages, see this essay.

[3] Information on the sensitivity of TATP and how it is not typically searched for via explosive detection screening can be viewed in "Triacetone Triperoxide (TATP)." GlobalSecurity.org. 7 July 2011, http://www.globalsecurity.org/military/systems/munitions/tatp.htm.

[4] Another variation of these masked explosive devices are those secreted in common objects such as in musical instruments, TV video cameras, and even a watermelon.

[5] These were Flight No. 1353 Volga-Avta Express and Flight No. 1047 Siberia Airlines. See "TSA's John Pistole: On Women, Patdowns, & Bra Bombers." *Christian Science Monitor*. 22 November 2010, https://www.youtube.com/watch?v=60lq0-Pt_fQ. These incidents took place in 2004 not 2006. See also Department of Homeland Security, Office of General Inspector, Review of the Transportation Security Administration's Use of Pat-Downs in Screening Procedures (Redacted). OIG-06-10. November 2005, http://www.oig.dhs.gov/assets/Mgmt/OIGr_06-10_Nov05.pdf.

[6] For aviation security concerns and general background and analyses of these devices, see Robert J. Bunker, "Body Cavity Bombs: fantasy or reality?" *Aviation Security International*. No. 20., Vol. 5. October 2014: 16-18, 20, 22 and Robert J. Bunker and Christopher Flaherty, *Body Cavity Bombers: The New Martyrs—A Terrorism Research Center Book*. Bloomington: iUniverse, 2013.

[7] For more information on these incidents, see Europol, SC5—Counterterrorism Unit, *The concealment of Improvised Explosive Devices (IEDs) in rectal cavities*. The Hague, 18 September 2010 and Rod Nordland, "Attacker in Afghanistan Hid Bomb in His Body." *The New York Times*. 8 June 2013, http://www.nytimes.com/2013/06/09/world/asia/attacker-in-afghanistan-hid-bomb-in-his-body.html?_r=0.

[8] Steven Aftergood, "Death is a Master from Palestine." *Secrecy News*. Vol. 2002, Iss. No. 54. 18 June 2002, http://fas.org/sgp/

news/secrecy/2002/06/061802.html. These allegations have become politicized with much debate associated with them.

[9] Robert A. Pape, Dying to Win: The Strategic Logic of Suicide Terrorism. New York: Random House, 2005: 226 and Sayed Salahuddin and Erin Cunningham, "Afghan president's cousin assassinated by suicide bomber." *The Washington Post.* 29 July 2014, http://www.washingtonpost.com/world/asia_pacific/afghan-presidents-cousin-assassinated-by-suicide-bomber/2014/07/29/7fccf124-1714-11e4-9e3b-7f2f110c6265_story.html.

[10] Such explosive research is a component of larger military nanotechnology programs that have been going on for years now. See Michael Berger, "Military nanotechnology: high precision explosives through nanoscale structuring." Nanowerk. 5 June 2008, http://www.nanowerk.com/spotlight/spotid=5956.php.

[11] One dedicated meeting related to this topic and body cavity smuggling itself is the upcoming Body Search 2015 event set in London in June, http://bodysearchworld.com. Advanced internal body screening technologies will be presented at this forum.

Further Readings

Robert J. Bunker, *The Projected Al Qaeda Use of Body Cavity Suicide Bombs Against High Value Targets.* Occasional Paper. GroupIntel Network. March 2011: 1-54, https://www.oodaloop.com/wp-content/uploads/2011/04/Bunker-GroupIntel_BodyCavityBombs.pdf.

Robert J. Bunker and Christopher Flaherty, Editors, *Body Cavity Bombers: The New Martyrs—A Terrorism Research Center Book.* Bloomington: iUniverse, 2013: 1-362.

Robert J. Bunker, "The Evolution of Terrorist Bombings." *Front Line Defence.* Vol. 11., No. 4. 2014, https://defence.frontline. online/article/2014/5/142-The-Evolution-of-Terrorist-Bombings.

Essay 5

Use and Potentials of Counter-Optical Lasers in Riots and Terrorism

This essay in the Terrorism Futures series focuses on LASER (Light Amplification by Stimulated Emission of Radiation) effects on human vision and activities in the context of riots and terrorism. Both the use and potentials of counter-optical lasers—that is, lasers utilized so as to disrupt and degrade human vision—will be highlighted with in regard to each of these forms of criminal-political activities. Additionally, a discussion of some of the applicable police and security response (countermeasures) to such laser use will be provided.

Counter-Optical Lasers

Lasers have been around since the early 1960s and have found applications across numerous scientific, industrial, commercial, educational and military applications. Other than in laser lightshows and in science fiction films, the general public was not typically exposed to lasers until the advent of laser pointers—initially, red ones and, as the technology matured and the prices drastically fell, the much brighter green ones [1]. As a result, lasers have been ubiquitous since the 1990s with present uses including barcode scanning, highlighting presentations, firearms sighting, and even as amusing cat toys. The projected 2015 market for these devices is now approaching $10 billion dollars for the year [2].

Counter-optical lasers refer to lasers directed against biological optics (typically human eyes) and electro-mechanical devices. Relatively few dedicated counter-optical lasers actually exist as opposed to the millions of other laser devices—most commonly laser pointers—yet, when they do, they have been specifically designed for policing and military purposes. When used by police, such devices are meant to disrupt vision but do not typically harm the eyes of the human being targeted. The same goes for such devices used by the military in policing-like operational environments. However, far more powerful military devices that can neutralize opposing force electro-mechanical optics (and as collateral damage do severe injury to the eyes of soldiers utilizing them) also exist [3].

Hence, laser pointers like most other types of laser devices, including the many more powerful ones, essentially become counter-optical lasers when directed at human eyes. This use typically takes place under nighttime conditions when pupils are more dilated and susceptible to bright light. Thus even low energy lasers, as opposed to industrial and military high energy lasers that can cut through materials or shoot down rockets respectively, are able to disrupt and degrade human vision along with negating those activities associated with it across a spectrum of increasingly severe levels of impaction.

Effects on Vision and Other Activities

At the most basic level, shining a laser at an individual can cause a startle reaction in the target which could conceivably result in injury to a driver or someone engaging in a dangerous task if it struck at the wrong moment. Also an individual may see a telltale 'red dot' placed on their chest that could raise personal safety concerns such as being sighted by a weapon. As a result, the anxiety level of the person so illuminated may immediately be raised.

The next level of disruption is that of distraction and annoyance with the laser light being shined into one's eyes. This can increase to a glare effect—similar to after of looking into the sun—if greater brightness is encountered. Tearing and watering of the eyes can then ensue if prolonged illumination takes place along with an eye burning sensation. At this point, vision is degraded, if not totally inhibited, with greater levels of severity resulting in flash blindness and afterimage effects and even eye pain. If enough energy gets into the human eye (which has a quarter second blink and aversion defensive reflex mechanism), actual corneal or even retinal damage may take place via different biological processes [4]. Luckily, most lasers encountered are of the eye safe variety and will not normally damage the eyes should one be illuminated.

Depending on the length and intensity of the lasing taking place, the effects on one's activities can be minimal through severe on the scale of visual disruption effects. It should be noted that magnifying optics—such as eyeglasses, binoculars, and conventional gun scopes—should be considered hazardous to use in a laser threat environment. They can intensify laser energy directed into the human eye and thus cause far more serious damage to an individual being illuminated by a laser beam than would normally occur. Highly reflective objects such as SWAT tactical mirrors should also not be utilized under such conditions due to specular reflection effects. Windshields and helicopter canopies also produce unique challenges when struck by lasers due to the micro-abrasions they contain, potentially resulting in opaque barriers that cannot be viewed through.

Laser devices can also be directed at security cameras to temporarily "blind" them (if targeted with weak lasers) and even potentially burn them out (when much stronger lasers are being utilized). Higher energy lasers can create a crazed glass effect in electro-optics or even start fires—though encountering such lasers in criminal and terrorist incidents would presently be an extreme rarity.

Use and Potentials in Riots

Laser pointers were first noted used in the 'Battle for Seattle' in November 1999 in Seattle, Washington when protestors (mainly anarchists) utilized them against responding police during the WTO (World Trade Organization) demonstrations. These were weak 'red' laser pointers and only caused very limited visual disruptive effects. While some discussions of laser use potentials were raised in various anarchist media following this incident and in Genoa, Italy in July 2001 an operation was even put in place to utilize 1,000 cheap mirrors for counter-optical purposes (during the G8 summit), it was roughly nine years before lasers were once again utilized in noticeable numbers in a riot type situation [5].

In December 2008 in Athens, Greece, far brighter 'green' lasers were utilized against riot control police in ongoing street battles with protestors who also hurled eggs, rocks, and Molotov cocktails [6]. Lasers have been used individually and in small clusters against police officers with between a half-dozen to a dozen evident in large demonstrations and subsequently directed against Greek governmental buildings. The use of such laser devices has continued in violent Greek austerity protests ever since with their use readily evident in June 2011, February 2012, and March 2015 [7].

Counter-optical laser use was also evident in the December 2012 and February 2013 protests and street battles in Egypt and even more so in the mass Egyptian demonstrations that took place in Cairo in June/July 2013. In the later protests dozens of green lasers were seen striking Egyptian military helicopters circling over Tahrir Square, demonstrating an escalation of use. A few of the newer and extremely bright 'blue' lasers also appear evident in some of the incident photos [8]. Besides targeting the military craft, lasers were also directed against governmental buildings, police, and, at times, opposing protestors throughout the months of civil strife.

For protestors and rioters, lasers offer superior 'less lethal' standoff capabilities against police forces that result in officer vision disruption and inability to perform certain tasks and an area denial capability in the case of air assets. These devices are increasingly being used in larger and larger groupings with the expectation, derived from the mass Egyptian demonstrations, that dozens of such devices may now be encountered in civil unrest scenarios.

Use and Potentials in Terrorism

Terrorists, insurgents, and organized criminals have had an on-again and off-again interest in using counter-optical lasers since the mid-1990s. The earliest known interest in using lasers for terrorism purposes can be traced back to the Aum Shinrikyo cult in Japan. This group had a proclivity for high tech and exotic weapons—like sarin gas and drones—and sought Russian scientific help in furthering the cult's research into laser weapons. In October 1994, the group built a truck mounted red gas laser that malfunctioned during the testing stage. The intent was to possibly utilize the laser against Tokyo policemen. Following this failed attempt, the cult then tried to purchase a half-million dollar laser system from a California company to no avail just prior to their Tokyo sarin attack [9].

Two incidents then took place a few days apart in October 1998 near Zenica and Tuzla, Bosnia. Counter-optical lasers were utilized by Serbian forces against U.S. helicopters, causing minor injuries to at least one of the flight crews. Based upon the circumstances of the incidents, military-grade lasers were likely involved such as non-eye safe rangefinders or illuminators. US helicopters were grounded in those areas of operations for about a week until protective laser eyewear could then be provided to the threatened aircrews [10].

In January 2002 near Fabens, Texas a US border patrol helicopter was struck by a red (or near infrared) laser coming across the border from Mexico. The laser beam originated from a vehicle belonging to individuals dressed like Mexican military personnel next to a known stash house. Given the location of the incident, it is quite likely that the perpetrators may have been Zetas, former Mexican special forces members in the pay of the Gulf cartel. The border patrol helicopter was forced to leave the area due to the intensity of the beam, likely a laser rangefinder, but fortunately the crew did not suffer any eye damage [11].

In November 2004, the FBI (Federal Bureau of Investigation) and DHS (Department of Homeland Security) issued a national bulletin that Al Qaeda or other terrorist groups might try to use lasers as weapons against aircraft [12]. This was followed in 2006 with concerns raised over radical Islamists on a forum discussing the idea of using lasers, especially green ones, against fighter jets. One participant even suggested providing laser pointers to children to aim at the jets, and another stated that they had utilized a single laser against two commercial jets forcing them to return to an airport [13].

While the validity of the last statement may be suspect— though both helicopter and commercial airliner craft have been forced to land from low energy laser strikes in some rare circumstances [14]—the terrorist potentials of the more powerful counter-optical laser devices is very real. In fact, laser weaponry offers many advantages over traditional firearms and munitions stemming from its superior capabilities: speed of light, extreme standoff ranges, no ballistics, deep clip, and other attributes. While some mention of radical Islamist forum discussions on terrorism laser use potentials have been mentioned as late as 2014, terrorist interest in such devices presently appears to be at the off-again level. This partially stems from the fact that most terrorists are still conventional in orientation and remain focused on the knife, gun, or bomb for their attacks.

Police and Security Forces Response

Awareness and training represent the cornerstone of domestic security response to the use of lasers in riots and terrorism. Specific TTPs (tactics, techniques, and procedures) can be taught to responding officers, and even commercial pilots, along with the provision of protective eyewear as warranted. These tactics can be even as basic as using a simple clipboard to help block a laser illumination being directed at a pilot or riot control officer.

Procedures and systems also exist to help individuals be alerted to a laser strike and even trace one back to its point of origin. Initially device 'glow down' after use readily gave away the position of the perpetrator but most newer systems do not provide this signature so FLIR (forward looking infrared) and laser tracking and position identifying technologies may be required. Further, given the extreme standoff ranges of many counter-optical lasers, some sort of response capability based on the premise of fighting light with light should be considered utilizing white light (powerful spotlights mounted on helicopters) and eye safe law enforcement and military dazzling laser systems.

Ultimately, restrictions on the sales of certain lasers devices can also be implemented as well as enacting and updating criminal statues on laser use against law enforcement officers, public officials, and various forms of transportation (e.g. against drivers and pilots). Public awareness campaigns concerning the dangers of irresponsible laser use and the penalties involved for committing such crimes should also be made known. While such statues and media campaigns may not deter would-be terrorists from attempting to utilize lasers for criminal-political purposes, they may help to deter at least some individuals from utilizing them in violent demonstrations and riot control type situations or even stop some commercial aviation illuminations that might have taken place due to sheer ignorance [15].

Notes

[1] This is because "the human eye is about 50 times more sensitive to green light at 532 nm than to red light at 640 nm." See *Laser Pointer Safety Factsheet*. Environmental Health & Safety, University of California Irvine, n.d., https://www.ehs. uci.edu/programs/radiation/Laser%20Pointer%20Safety%20 Factsheet.pdf.

[2] Gail Overton et al., "Laser Marketplace 2015: Lasers surround us in the Year of Light." *Laser Focus World*. 16 January 2015, http://www.laserfocusworld.com/articles/print/volume-51/issue-01/features/laser-marketplace-2015-lasers-surround-us-in-the-year-of-light.html.

[3] For information on the international ban on laser weapons meant to blind humans, see *Protocol on Blinding Laser Weapons (Protocol IV to the 1980 Convention), 13 October 1995.* International Committee of the Red Cross, n.d., https://www.icrc.org/ihl/INTRO/570 and *Ban on blinding laser weapons now in force.* 30-07-1998 News Release 98/31. International Committee of the Red Cross, https://www.icrc.org/eng/resources/documents/misc/57jpa8.htm.

[4] For background information, see "Laser Bio-effects." *Berkeley Lab*. 2 February 2015, http://www2.lbl.gov/ehs/safety/lasers/bioeffects.shtml and Van B. Nakagawara, et al., "Laser Hazards In Navigable Airspace." *Federal Aviation Administration*. N.d., https://www.faa.gov/pilots/safety/pilotsafetybrochures/media/laser_hazards_web.pdf.

[5] Robert J. Bunker, "Counter-Optical Laser Use Against Law Enforcement in Athens." *Red Team Journal*. 23 February 2009, http://redteamjournal.com/2009/02/counter-optical-laser-use-against-law-enforcement-in-athens/.

[6] "Greek rioters use lasers against police as violence over boy's death continues into second week." *The Daily Mail*. 15 December 2008, http://www.dailymail.co.uk/news/article-1094892/Greek-rioters-use-lasers-police-violence-boys-death-continues-second-week.html.

[7] Dominic Sandbrook, "A crisis that could tear Europe apart." *The Daily Mail.* 17 June 2011, http://www.dailymail. co.uk/debate/article-2004550/Greece-riots-2011-A-crisis-tear-Europe-apart.html, "Greece: Laser pointers continue to be used in riots." *LaserPointerSafety.com.* 20 February 2012, http://www.laserpointersafety.com/news/news/nonaviation-incidents_files/9826caaf1bb6ada16752c60c690fa8c2-221.php, and Reuters, "Masked youths hurl stones and use a green laser beam during clashes with riot police in Athens." *Thompson Reuters Foundation.* 17 Match 2015, http://www.trust.org/item/20150317211036-ack4p/.

[8] Ryan Craggs, "Egyptian Protesters Bombard Helicopter With Lasers (PHOTOS)." *The Huffington Post.* 1 July 2013, http://www.huffingtonpost.com/2013/07/01/helicopter-laser-photos-egypt-protesters_n_3528371.html and "Egypt crisis: Why are Cairo protesters using laser pens?" *Magazine Monitor BBC News.* 4 July 2013, http://www.bbc.com/news/blogs-magazine-monitor-23178484.

[9] Robert J. Bunker, "Terrorists and Laser Weapons Use." *Studies in Conflict and Terrorism.* Vol. 1, No. 5. May 2008: 444.

[10] Ibid: 445.

[11] Ibid: 445. Infrared laser devices represent a whole new dimension to laser threat potentials and offer a number of unique advantages for terrorist use.

[12] Associated Press, "Terrorists May Use Lasers to Blind Pilots, FBI Warns." *Los Angeles Times.* 10 December 2004, http://articles.latimes.com/2004/dec/10/nation/na-lasers10.

[13] "Mujahideen Use Laser Pointers to Disrupt Fighter Jets." Islamist Websites Monitor No. 16. *MEMRI*. 31 October 2006, http://www.memrijttm.org/mujahideen-use-laser-pointers-to-disrupt-fighter-jets.html.

[14] Literally thousands of incidents in which commercial aircraft in the United States have been illuminated by lasers—the vast majority of which have been laser pointers—have taken place with only a minority of aircraft immediately forced to land. Still, the FBI is increasingly becoming concerned about such domestic US lasing incidents. See, for instance, "FBI Launches National Campaign to Address Laser Threat to Aircraft." National Press Releases. *Federal Bureau of Investigation Website*. 3 June 2014, http://www.fbi.gov/news/pressrel/press-releases/fbi-launches-national-campaign-to-address-laser-threat-to-aircraft.

[15] For response and counterterrorism protocols, see for example Matt Begert, "Laser Countermeasures." John P. Sullivan, Ed., *Jane's Unconventional Weapons Handbook*. London: Jane's Information Group, 2000: 229-235, Matt Begert, Lisa Campbell, and Sid Heal, "Disruptive and Destructive Effects of Laser Illuminations." *FBI Law Enforcement Bulletin*. April 2008: 10-15, and Madelyn I. Sawyer and John P. Sullivan, "Laser Legal Issues: Prosecuting Perpetrators." *FBI Law Enforcement Bulletin*. April 2008: 18-21.

Further Readings

Robert J. Bunker, *Tactical Laser Devices and Weapons: Guidebook for Law Enforcement*. June 2002. El Segundo, CA: National Law Enforcement and Corrections Technology Center-West (NLECTC-West). LE Restricted.

Robert J. Bunker, "Terrorists and Laser Weapons Use." *Studies in Conflict and Terrorism*. Vol. 1, No. 5. May 2008: 434-455.

Robert J. Bunker, "Counter-Optical Laser Use Against Law Enforcement in Athens." *Red Team Journal*. 23 February 2009, http://redteamjournal.com/2009/02/counter-optical-laser-use-against-law-enforcement-in-athens/.

Image Gallery

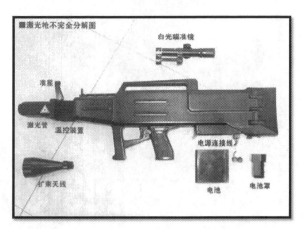

WJG-2002 Blinding Laser Gun. These weapons, including
the earlier ZM-87 produced by NORINCO, have been offered
on the international arms market and have the potential
to be acquired by terrorist organizations. The Ministry of
Defense, The People's Republic of China, 9 December 2015.
[For Public Distribution/No Restrictions on Use]

Al Sunnah Knights ("Jama'at Ansar al-Sunnah") Remote
Controlled Machine Gun Deployed in the Aleppo Region,
Syria in November 2012. Jama'at Ansar al-Sunnah Social
Media. [For Public Distribution/No Restrictions on Use]

Image Gallery

Image used by Digital Caliphate Supporters on Twitter. It Combines the Twitter Logo with the Flag of the Islamic State. Islamic State Social Media from June 2014.
[For Public Distribution/No Restrictions on Use]

White Power Pepe the Frog. Since mid-2016 Pepe imagery has been increasingly appropriated by Alt-Right and White Nationalist groups and affinity members. White Extremist Social Media.
[For Public Distribution/No Restrictions on Use]

Image Gallery

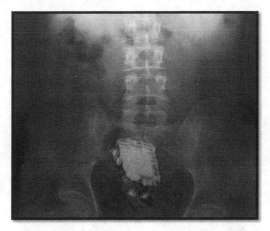

X-ray image of a cell phone hidden in the rectum of a prisoner in Sri Lanka in February 2013. Conceptual example of body cavity bomb deployment. Sri Lankan Government.
[For Public Distribution/No Restrictions on Use]

Chechen Government Headquarters Suicide Bombing, December 2002. Frame of the Attack from a Propaganda Video. Riyadus-Salikhin Reconnaissance and Sabotage Brigade Social Media.
[For Public Distribution/No Restrictions on Use]

Image Gallery

Explosives in the Bed of Daesh/IS AVBIED on Al Hawl Front, Northeastern Syria. Captured by Kurdish Yekîneyên Parastina Gel (YPG), December 2015. YPG Social Media.
[For Public Distribution/No Restrictions on Use]

Armored HMMWV with Welded Ram/Plating and Rear Plating Used as VBIED. Utilized Against Shia Military Base in Western Iraq in October 2015. Islamic State Social Media.
[For Public Distribution/No Restrictions on Use]

Image Gallery

Daesh/IS AVBIED on Al Hawl Front, Northeastern Syria. Captured by Kurdish Yekîneyên Parastina Gel (YPG), December 2015. YPG Social Media. [For Public Distribution/No Restrictions on Use]

Image Gallery

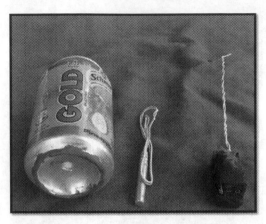

Image of the Purported Type of IED Utilized to Destroy a Russian Metrojet over the Sinai Peninsula in October 2015. "EXCLUSIVE – Image of the IED used to bring down the Russian airliner." Dabiq. Iss. 12, November 2015: 3. Islamic State Digital Media. [For Public Distribution/No Restrictions on Use]

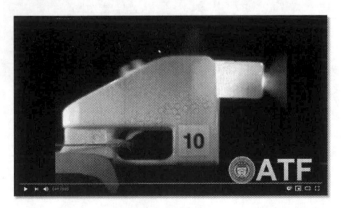

ATF test of 3-D printed firearm (Liberator) using ABS material (Side View). YouTube. 13 November 2013. ATFHQ Social Media. [For Public Distribution/No Restrictions on Use]

Image Gallery

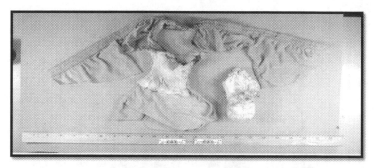

Image of the Underwear Bomb worn by Umar Farouk Abdulmutallab on 25 December 2009 on an international passenger airline flight from Amsterdam to Detroit. The explosive device failed to detonate. Federal Bureau of Investigation. [For Public Distribution/No Restrictions on Use]

Video frame capture from Christchurch First Person Shooter (FPS) Live Streaming Attack posted on Facebook by Brenton Tarrant a Right Wing (White Nationalist) Extremist. The image is of him approaching the doorway into a mosque on 15 March 2019 prior to his targeting of its worshipers. [For Public Distribution/No Restrictions on Use]

Image Gallery

The Ultimate Mowing Machine, in Inspire, Iss. 2,
October 2010: 53. Al Qaeda Digital Media.
[For Public Distribution/No Restrictions on Use]

Just Terror Tactics 3: Arson, in Rumiyah, Iss. 5,
January 2017: 8. Islamic State Digital Media.
[For Public Distribution/No Restrictions on Use]

Image Gallery

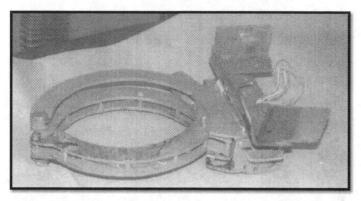

Image of the clamp and bracket (attached to a bomb) placed around the neck of Brian Douglas Wells who robbed a bank branch just outside Erie, Pennsylvania on 28 August 2003. When he was detained by state police following the robbery, the bomb exploded, killing him instantly. ERIE, PENNSYLVANIA MURDER-BOMBING MYSTERY: Information Sought. Federal Bureau of Investigation. 3 September 2003. [For Public Distribution/No Restrictions on Use]

Image of the clamp locking device (attached to a bomb) placed around the neck of Brian Douglas Wells who robbed a bank branch just outside Erie, Pennsylvania on 28 August 2003. When he was detained by state police following the robbery, the bomb exploded, killing him instantly. ERIE, PENNSYLVANIA MURDER-BOMBING MYSTERY: Information Sought. Federal Bureau of Investigation. 3 September 2003. [For Public Distribution/No Restrictions on Use]

Essay 6

Home Made, Printed, and Remote Controlled Firearms—Terrorism and Insurgency Implications

This essay in the Terrorism Futures series focuses on trends in the manufacturing of homemade and printed firearms along with the emergence of remote (teleoperated) firearms. Each of these trends is discussed in turn in this short essay, as are the implications of their cumulative effects on terrorism and insurgency. Ultimately, as will be highlighted in this piece, both physical and cyber forms of terrorism are increasingly merging as a result of firearm and computer components becoming more closely integrated [1].

Home Made Firearms

In October 2014, Jalisco's Attorney General stated that two clandestine arms factories in Guadalajara, Mexico linked to the Cártel de Jalisco Nueva Generación (CJNG) were raided by Mexican authorities in cooperation with the US government [2]. This is the same violent cartel responsible for ambushing scores of Mexican police officers, closing down entire cities with burning car and bus roadblocks and mass building arson, and even, in May 2015, shooting down a Mexican military helicopter with rocket propelled grenades (RPGs).

Two converted residences—the first of their kind ever discovered in Mexico—were used to assemble AR-15 assault rifle components purchased legally online with no background checks in the United States. Parts of homemade guns can be purchased in this manner as long as the receivers—the mechanical part which cycles, fires, and ejects the bullets—are only about 80% partially built. Such unfinished receivers were then completed in these underground weapons factories by specialized milling machines and fitted to other AR-15 components to create well over a hundred finished firearms prior to their being shutdown [3]. Such an off-the-books firearm has no production serial number or original registered owner to trace it back to and, for all intents and purposes, thus really does not even exist.

The emerging trend towards the production of homemade assault rifles, derived from unfinished parts, has until recently been largely unrecognized. A particular gun parts seller with one store in California and another in Florida estimated that they would sell about 75,000 unfinished receivers in 2014 alone. Such clean—that is non-serialized and unregistered—weapons are increasingly being used by gang members in the United States and by criminal organizations and the cartels throughout parts of Latin America including Mexico and Colombia. To date, hundreds of such finished AR-15 and AK-47 style weapons have been recovered by the US ATF alone [4]. Such weapons, however, do not appear to have as of yet proliferated to more traditional terrorist and insurgent groups such as Al Qaeda and Islamic State. This is likely the case because those groups tend to operate in conflict environments in which black market arms are relatively easy to obtain. Further, they are also able to readily engage in outright governmental arsenal seizures as has taken place in Iraq, Syria, and Yemen whenever the opportunity presents itself.

Still, the severity of this homemade guns assembly issue has now resulted in the release of ATF Rul. 2015-1 in January 2015 that addresses the '80% receivers' legal loophole [5]. Whether this ruling will also help to facilitate the eventual shutdown of online sales of such receivers and gun kits from non-US online sellers is unknown. However, 3D printing technology is rapidly advancing to the point that purchasing gun parts online for home assembly will one day become obsolete anyway. Such trending operates in much the same way that internet music downloads have replaced earlier sales of physically based compact disc (CD) music.

Printed Firearms

The first 3D plastic printed gun—'The Liberator'—was created in May 2013. It was a single shot pistol design with a very limited operational lifespan [6]. Soon after that gun was printed—with 100,000 online printing files downloaded by the general public prior to the computer schematics being taken down by the US government—a long series of printed guns were produced that were cheaper to create and more durable and functional in their design. In July 2013, the first printed plastic rifle was produced [7] and, by November 2013, a metal 1911 .45 Caliber pistol was printed [8]. In 2014, special bullets designed for 3D printed guns were then created, and, in 2015, a much heavier Colt Cm901 7.62mm assault rifle had been printed along with a metal silencer [9]. Additional 3D printing breakthroughs are expected to continue to take place.

Printed gun advances—along with the initial printing of plastic AR-15 receivers as has already taken place—may soon create a synergy with CNC milling technology. As early as September 2014, computer milling allowed for finished aluminum AR-15 receivers to be produced in sizeable quantities by a $1,200.00 CNC mill known as the 'Ghost Gunner' [10]. While no mention of the 3D metal printing of AR-15 receivers has been noted, it is only a matter of time of before this capability is achieved. Combined with cheap CNC mills and the ability to print all AR-15 components in metal, the new ATF Rul. 2015-1 will pretty much become meaningless.

As would be expected, 3D printing had caught the attention of 'early adaptor' criminals as early as 2011 with designs on printing plastic car and handcuff keys and high capacity assault rifle magazines [11]. It was initially thought that the first illicit 3D printed gun factory had been raided in Manchester, United Kingdom in October 2013, but this turned out to be unfounded [12]. An illicit 3D firearm printing operation was actually discovered in May 2014 in Japan belonging to an individual subsequently charged with criminal possession of multiple firearms [13]. More incidents have taken place with what appear to be plastic 3D printed gun parts belonging to a drug dealer being seized in Australia in 2015 [14].

While concerns over potentials for terrorists printing weapons have been made known by governmental and police officials in multiple countries and many 3D weapons printing bans have been enacted, no known incidents in which terrorists or insurgents have printed firearms have as of yet have been identified [15]. This is likely due to the same reasons that such groups are not yet assembling home made firearms—it is presently much simpler and easier to either purchase them on the black market or raid police and military weapons depots and steal them. Still, the trending potentials are clear, as is the rapidly evolving nature of these weapons. In fact, the next frontier for 3D printing will be that of remote operated systems where by gun parts will be printed with integrated computer circuits to create hybrid firearm-computer systems. This leads us to our next firearms technology use trend.

Remote Controlled Firearms

Concerns over terrorist use of teleoperated (remote) firearms that can be physically fired in one location while the operator is in another location have existed for over well over a decade now. Initially these were notional and science fiction derived perceptions, however, contemporary advances in technology and actual incidents in which they have been used have now made these viable concerns. While a remotely fired sniper rifle set up in a bell tower mimicking the August 1966 University of Texas massacre sans the physical presence of the shooter may seem a stretch of the imagination, this is now easily achievable for terrorist utilization.

The initial indication of the possibility of remote firearm use potentials by terrorists took place with the development of the Live-Shot virtual hunting system. The system was marketed by a Texas company so that disabled hunters could shoot Whitetail Deer. Conceived as early as 2003 and created in 2005 after an investment of about $15,000, the system consisted of a rifle mounted on a motorized platform controlled by a computer linked to the internet. A remote user, utilizing their own computer system via the internet in another location, could control the operation of the rifle—the aiming and firing of it—in real time via a camera link [16]. Immediate backlash against the system took place due to public outrage, with a resulting widespread ban on internet hunting in the United States since being enacted [17].

While the Live-Shot system turned out to be a failed business venture, conceptually the ability to aim and shoot a firearm via an internet linked computer was proven beyond a doubt. All that was then required was to change the intended target from a deer to a human. This took place by at least 2013 with the TRAP T192 Remote Sniper Kit being commercially offered by a security products company for both ambush and counter-sniper applications. The kit comes with solar-powered battery charging that allows for weapons system placement loitering capability [18]. That same year, a Wi-Fi capable precision guided firearm (PGF) was also offered commercially by a different company. It allowed a user with a smart phone or tablet to activate, via a unique PIN system, a computer guided aiming system that offers trained sniper equivalent targeting capabilities [19]. No actual instances of the use of these systems in media reports have been noted [20].

Actual battlefield use did take place in March 2013 and July 2014 by FSA (Free Syrian Army) fighters utilizing remote controlled sniper rifles. This fielding of two improvised systems occurred in Syria with videos of their use placed on online social media. In both instances, a short control cable from the weapon is connected to a user with a small tablet/controller around an interior corner of a building so that counter-sniper fires will not target them. In the latter video, the weapon is being fired unlike in the initial video [21]. A video posting in June 2013 of a FSA remote controlled machine gun being fired has also surfaced [22]. Purported Islamic State affinity chats have since taken place in January 2015 related to the 'remote control technique' (translated from Arabic) for firing weapons [23]. Combined with a recent discussion of the Ansar al-Islam use of a remote-controlled truck with a machine gun bed mount [24], this would suggest that both terrorist and insurgent organizations are beginning to become well aware that remote control firearm technologies exist and offer unique tactical battlefield applications.

Terrorism and Insurgency Implications

The above firearms trends can be viewed as a compliment to homemade IED manufacturing and remote detonation that have existed for decades now. Basically, a more discriminate point—and to some extent area—firearms targeting capability is emerging to compliment the earlier non-discriminate area targeting capability that has long existed with smaller IED and larger VBIED use. This will result in new terrorist and insurgent capabilities eventually being gained in the areas of:

- *Remote Sniping*—the shooter is both protected from harm (has removed himself or herself from the battlefield) and, via a stabilized platform and computerized aiming system, is able to engage in the precision engagement of point targets like a sniper.
- *Virtual Targeting Presence*—that is, having the ability to threaten potential targets in a specific area for long durations by means of remote sensing overwatch. Additionally, proximity and motion detector alerts that notify the remote firearm user of any human activity 24/7 can be utilized for longer extended periods of time.
- *Remote Combined Arms*—creating interlocking remote-controlled fields of fire with remote detonated IEDs for both offensive terrorist targeting purposes and defensive channeling and urban kill zone utilization by insurgent forces.

These homemade, printed, and remote-controlled trends are also resulting in firearm and computer integration for both weapon manufacturing and utilization needs. This experimental merging of firearm and computer has been progressing in fits and starts for a while now. It can be seen in the initial next generation U.S. conventional military systems attempt via the OICW (Objective Individual Combat Weapon)—with its onboard computer utilized for grenade round air bursting solution calculations—that would have engaged opposing forces in defilade positions that are protected from direct fires.

As described in the earlier sections, terrorist and insurgent organizations will also benefit from the self-manufacturing of firearms as a means to bypass black market weapons constraints—especially in states with strong anti-arms smuggling regimes—as well as in the repair of broken firearms with the metal printing of precision replacement parts.

While none of these implications will significantly alter the 'disruptive' and 'terror' generating components of terrorism itself, they may alter some of its weapons procurement logistical requirements and potentially even allow for the generation of greater numbers of casualties during a specific terrorist incident while at the same time greatly reducing terrorist casualties in return. Additionally, such incidents would likely help to blur our understanding of both physical and cyber forms of terrorism, as they presently exist. This would result in unique counterterrorism dilemmas being created that would ultimately require new and innovative response and intelligence protocols being developed by police and state security forces.

Notes

[1] For a short primer on humanspace and cyberspace dimensionality, see Robert J. Bunker, "Fifth Dimensional

Battlespace: Terrorism and Counter-Terrorism Implications." *TRENDS Research & Advisory*. 10 February 2015, http:// trendsinstitution.org/?p=1004.

[2] The original announcement in Spanish can be found at "Fábrica de armas del Cártel Jalisco Nueva Generación." *YouTube*. Posted 7 October 2014, https://www.youtube.com/ watch?v=XVCfGsOgLkc.

[3] David Gagne, "Clandestine Arms Factories Discovered in Mexico." *InsightCrime*. 8 October 2014, http://www. insightcrime.org/news-briefs/first-arms-manufacturing-lab-discovered-in-mexico and Mauricio Ferrer, "Desmantelan "fábrica" de armas y aseguran a 4 traficantes y cien cuernos de chivo en Jalisco." *La Jornada*. 7 Octubre 2014, http:// www.jornada.unam.mx/ultimas/2014/10/07/desmantelan-201cfabrica201d-de-armas-y-aseguran-a-4-traficantes-y-cien-cuernos-de-chivo-en-jalisco-3565.html. Also see Alissa Figueroa, "Increasing Number of Homemade Guns Being Used to Kill." *Fusion*. 15 April 2014, http://fusion.net/story/5286/increasing-number-of-homemade-guns-being-used-to-kill/. See the 7:54 minute video that accompanies this article.

[4] Alissa Figueroa, "Increasing Number of Homemade Guns Being Used to Kill."

[5] "ATF Rul. 2015-1." U.S. Department of Justice, Bureau of Alcohol, Tobacco, Firearms and Explosives, Office of the Director. 2 January 2015, https://www.atf.gov/file/11711/ download.

[6] Andy Greenberg, "Meet The 'Liberator': Test-Firing The World's First Fully 3D-Printed Gun." *Forbes*. 5 May 2013,

http://www.forbes.com/sites/andygreenberg/2013/05/05/meet-the-liberator-test-firing-the-worlds-first-fully-3d-printed-gun/ and the "Defense Distributed website," https://defdist.org.

[7] Andy Greenberg, "How 3-D Printed Guns Evolved Into Series Weapons In Just One Year." *Wired*. 15 May 2014, http://www.wired.com/2014/05/3d-printed-guns/ and Adam Clark Estes, "3D-Printed Guns Are Only Getting Better, and Scarier." *Gizmodo*. 6 January 2015, http://gizmodo.com/3d-printed-guns-are-only-getting-better-and-scarier-1677747439.

[8] "World's First 3D Printed Gun." *Solid Concepts Blog*. 7 November 2013, https://blog.solidconcepts.com/industry-highlights/worlds-first-3d-printed-metal-gun/.

[9] See Andy Greenberg, "The Bullet That Could Make 3-D Printed Guns Practical Deadly Weapons." *Wired*. 5 November 2014, http://www.wired.com/2014/11/atlas-314-3-d-printed-guns-bullets/, Dan Kedmey, "Now 3D-Printed Guns Can Fire Even Bigger Bullets." *Time*. 27 March 2015, http://time.com/3761456/3d-printed-gun-nato-rounds/, and Scott J. Grunewald, "North America Just Tested Its First Functional Metal 3D Printed Gun Silencer." *3DPrint*. 7 April 2015, http://3dprint.com/56493/metal-3d-printed-gun-silencer/.

[10] Andy Greenberg, "The $1,200 Machine That Lets Anyone Make a Metal Gun at Home." *Wired*. 1 October 2014, http://www.wired.com/2014/10/cody-wilson-ghost-gunner/ and the "Ghost Gunner website," https://ghostgunner.net.

[11] David Daw, "Criminals Find New Uses for 3D Printing." *PC World*. 10 October 2011, http://www.pcworld.com/

article/241605/criminals find new uses for 3d printing. html.

[12] Chris Greenwood, James Slack, and Wills Robinson, "Police raid 'Britain's first 3D gun factory': Officers seize printer they believe criminals were using to make firearms." *Daily Mail*. 25 October 2013, http://www.dailymail.co.uk/news/article-2476392/Police-raid-Britains-3D-gun-factory-Officers-seize-printer-believe-criminals-using-make-firearms.html and Adam Clark Estes, "UK Police Seize 3D-Printed Gun Parts That Are Actually 3D Printer Parts." *Gizmodo*. 25 October 2011, http://gizmodo.com/uk-police-seize-3d-printed-gun-parts-that-are-actually-1452087573.

[13] "Japan man held over '3D-printed guns.'" *BBC News*. 8 May 2014, http://www.bbc.com/news/technology-27322947.

[14] "3D-printed weapons found during Australian police raid." *de zeen magazine*. 11 February 2015, http://www.dezeen.com/2015/02/11/3d-printed-weapons-found-australian-police-raid-gold-coast-queensland/.

[15] See, for example, Sarah Anderson, "UK Police Note Potential for 3D Printing Uses in Terrorist Activity." *3D Print*. 27 April 2015, http://3dprint.com/59830/uk-anti-terror-3d-printing/.

[16] See "A Virtual Long Shot: Hunting Texas Whitetails from a Computer." *Field & Stream*. N.d., http://www.fieldandstream.com/node/1005010612 and Sylvia Moreno, "Mouse Click Brings Home Thrill of the Hunt." *The Washington Post*. 8 May 2005, http://www.washingtonpost.com/wp-dyn/content/article/2005/05/07/AR2005050701270.html.

[17] For early information on the banning of internet hunting and its implementation in 35 US states, see Veronica Rose and Gerald Barrett, *Internet Hunting*. OLR Research Report. 2008-R-0129. 19 February 2008, http://www.cga.ct.gov/2008/rpt/2008-r-0129.htm.

[18] Richard Johnson, "Precision Remotes TRAP T192 Remote Sniper Kit." *The Fire Arm Blog*. 18 October 2013, http://www.thefirearmblog.com/blog/2013/10/18/precisionremotes-trap-t192-remote-sniper-kit/. The company website is at http://www.precisionremotes.com.

[19] Paul Marks, "'Self-aiming' rifle turns novices into expert snipers." *New Scientist*. 21 May 2013, http://www.newscientist.com/article/dn23571-selfaiming-rifle-turns-novices-into-expert-snipers.html#.VV9spUuIzFI. The company website at http://tracking-point.com presently states "Due to financial difficulty TrackingPoint will no longer be accepting orders."

[20] While it is assumed that only legitimate governmental, law enforcement, and associated entities may purchase these remote-controlled systems, the actual vetting process has not been determined.

[21] Spencer Ackerman, "Video: Syrian Rebel Jury-Rigs A Remote Controlled Rifle." *Wired*. 27 March 2013, http://www.wired.com/2013/03/syria-remote-control/ and "*[HQ] The Remote Controlled Sniper-Rifle Is Back For Action#*." *LiveLeak*. 29 July 2014, http://www.liveleak.com/view?i=99c_1406651450.

[22] "Raw Video FSA Machine Gun." *YouTube*. 2 June 2013, https://www.youtube.com/watch?v=k6O98j3z9so#t=19.

[23] Tribune Media Jihadist Forum. "Islamic State made sniper mechanism operates by remote control." (Translation from Arabic). January https://www.mnbr.info/vb/archive/index. php/t-77386.html.

[24] Marc Goodman, "How Terrorists Are Turning Robots Into Weapons." *Defense One.* 16 April 2005, http://www.defenseone.com/ideas/2015/04/how-terrorists-are-turning-robots-weapons/110362/.

Further Readings

Robert J. Bunker and Alma Keshavarz, *Terrorist and Insurgent Teleoperated Sniper Rifles and Machine Guns.* Fort Leavenworth, KS: Foreign Military Studies Office (FMSO), August 2016: 1-40, https://community.apan.org/wg/tradoc-g2/fmso/m/fmso-monographs/194883.

C. Flaherty, "Employment of 3D-Printed Guns in the 5D Battlespace." *Journal of Information Warfare.* Vol 15, No 1. 2016: 29-43.

David A. Kuhn, Robert J. Bunker, and Alma Keshavarz, *Islamic State Teleoperated 73mm SPG-9 Recoilless Guns: Twin Mount.* Fort Leavenworth, KS: Foreign Military Studies Office (FMSO), July 2017: 1-11, https://community.apan.org/wg/tradoc-g2/fmso/m/fmso-monographs/200598.

Essay 7

The Use of Social Media Bots and Automated (AI Based) Text Generators—Key Technologies in Winning the Propaganda War Against Islamic State/Daesh?

This essay in the Terrorism Futures series will Islamic series will discuss Islamic State(IS)/Daesh's use of social media along with recent trends in commercial bot and automated text systems. It will then highlight the relationship of IS/Daesh to computer algorithms and similar bot-like applications in social media along with automated text generators. It will conclude with the implications these technology trends may likely have on IS/Daesh and on the international community response being directed against it. Ultimately, in such an increasingly computer science and artificial intelligence dominated conflict, IS/Daesh may find that replicating its early social media successes may now be extremely difficult.

IS/Daesh and Social Media

IS/Daesh has proven itself to be highly adept at using social media to promote its extremist ideology and expand into a global terrorism network that has displaced Al Qaida as the premier Sunni radical Islamist organization. Such media fulfills the need to widely communicate group activities, help radicalize dispersed communities of interest, raise funds online, and to ensure that a fresh supply of foot-soldiers replace those killed in airstrikes and ground offensives in Iraq and Syria [1]. Social media is also critically important to IS because it can be used for psychological and propaganda purposes—including the terrorizing of besieged towns—and can help to promote IS international branding and market share as the rightly guided stewards of reestablishing the Caliphate.

Recent reporting on IS/Daesh's use of Twitter suggests that in autumn 2014 this terrorist organization peaked with at least 45,000 accounts (an aggregate of both newly created and suspended accounts). The group had earlier developed the Arabic language 'The Dawn of Golden Tidings' (i.e. Dawn) app for Twitter for news group purposes and had also gained a mastery of hashtag use for tweet campaigns to obtain top trending tags which are then retweeted by the @ActiveHashtags stream [2].

IS/Daesh is an adaptive network and has seen almost 19,000 actual and suspected member Twitter accounts—mostly in English—closed as well as the shutdown of the Dawn app. As a result, since early 2015 it has shifted from English to Arabic as its dominant form of social media communication. Of course, the continued posting of pictures and audio-video imagery is still taking place—though now predominately in Arabic [3]. Additionally, due to the recognition of ongoing IS/

Daesh social media analysis by the international community, that terrorist organization has now placed malware triggers in its blogs. When Arabic text is translated into English and also Japanese via search engines such as Google and Bing, malware is released which infects the computer systems of unsuspecting researchers [4]. Additional types of related IS/Daesh malware countermeasures—such as keyboard loggers and remote access software—also exist based on other triggering protocols.

Social Media Bots and Automated Text Generators

As of August 2014, Twitter was said to have over 270 million users who are active and engage in tweets. Of these users, roughly 23 million are bots and apps utilized for humor, commercial spamming (e.g. advertising and promotional links), and malware and virus insertion purposes [5]. Bot creation is thus very prevalent with some websites—Swenzy and Fiverr, for instance—selling 'likes,' 'comments,' and 'followers' to social media accounts [6]. Other forms of social media such as Facebook have similar issues with 140 to 170 million fake— that is bot derived—profiles and users estimated out of roughly 1.49 billion accounts (i.e. accounts logged into in the last 30 days) [7].

Beyond these relatively basic bots and the bot nets that may, control them another level of computer science sophistication is beginning to have an influence on global social media. Automated text generators have developed within the last decade and are being spearheaded by a handful of high-tech companies. Two approaches are being undertaken for commercial purposes and are focused on exploiting structured data for mass news reporting and for book creation. In the news reporting realm, Narrative Sciences and Automated Insights dominate and have created AI systems that learn and benefit from 'meta-writer' templates (narrative shells and rules provided by subject matter experts such as journalists) which allows for the news text produced to be read by humans without them realizing that it is machine generated. In 2014, over a billion yearly sports updates of little league games and women's baseball, weather forecasts, corporate earnings reports, monthly franchise reports, and similar material are being produced in this manner with the Associated Press, Forbes.com, and other news agencies now utilizing such text generation services [8].

The book publishing utilization of these systems has been pioneered by Icon Group International for the mass consumer market and its application for internal corporate reports (like the monthly franchise reports noted earlier) and even the licensing of such proprietary AI has been vested with its subsidiary EdgeMaven Media [9]. Hundreds of thousands of formulaic books and other material have been created via this AI system which are both original and non-plagiaristic products but not necessarily creative in their approach. Essentially, the computer algorithms utilized scrape the internet of the specific topical content input via the parameters provided and then, using relational metrics and other heuristics and analytics, can quickly and cheaply create a book length product such as *The 2007-2012 World Outlook for Wood Toilet Seats*. Tables, figures, indexes, and imagery such as photographs can also be added to such products. While the book will likely sell very few copies at a price of $795.00, it only requires one sale to make a massive profit based on the fact it cost less than a dollar to generate [10]. Repeat the process within other specialized book niches hundreds of thousands—what in the future will become millions—of times and the commercial value of this approach becomes readily apparent. Competing systems such as Nimble

Book's PageKicker system also exist as well as the experimental European What-If Machine (WHIM) project [11].

IS/Daesh Use and Potentials

As seen in the preceding section, from a terrorist perspective bots and auto text generators can offer new social media influencing potentials. Focusing on bots first, our understanding of actual IS/Daesh use of social media bots, however, is very much more opaque than other social media sectors. A best estimate is simply that thousands of Twitter bots are being utilized. To a lesser extent, Al Qaida in the Arabian Peninsula (AQAP) and Al Nusra Front in Syria (an Al Qaida affiliate) are also employing such bots but have proven far less adept at their use [12]. Per the *ISIS Twitter Census* report produced by the Brookings Institution in March 2015, the IS/Daesh bot use strategy emerged after the demise of Dawn in June 2014 and is as follows:

> In the wake of that setback, ISIS supporters have responded by creating a large number of bots in small clusters, with each cluster using a different service to post tweets of the propaganda and hashtags it wishes to promote. If one "family" of bots is suspended, there are still many others that will continue to tweet. Thousands of such accounts were detected in the course of this analysis. Many from this new generation of bots were constructed using popular third party automation services such as IFTT (If This, Then That), which Twitter is unlikely to shut down since it is much more commonly used for innocuous purposes by ordinary users [13].

IS/Daesh tweets topped out at about 133,000 per day per the ISIS Twitter Census report. The census data set estimated that 20% or so of all tweets were generated by bots and apps. In a best case estimate, 26,000 daily tweets were non-human generated although, with IS/Daesh tweet capability degraded, the average daily level is now much lower [14].

This analysis suggests that IS/Daesh is presently in what can be termed the first phase of automated social media use—that is, using bots to rebroadcast pre-existing text, sound, and imagery. Even then, this is only a marginal capability compared to the massive volumes rebroadcast by the tens-of-millions of bots engaging in this practice within the commercialized and criminalized elements of social media. Still, this level of social media use—both human and machine generated—is causing international community concerns because of the ongoing effectiveness of online IS/Daesh radicalization efforts which have so far replaced their foot soldier casualties with new recruits.

When turning our attention to AI systems, no evidence has surfaced that IS/Daesh as an organization is presently aware of what can be termed the second phase of automated social media use—that is, the creation of new text, the proper utilization of imagery within that text, and even the expectation that audio-visual (e.g. video) products will at some point be created [15]. As highlighted earlier, this capability is presently only thought to be held by a handful of cutting edge corporations primarily seeking to make money in commercial news and book publishing markets—though the wider proliferation of this capability is ultimately unknown with the likelihood that the intelligence services of various states, and potentially even some of their proxies, already secretly possess it.

If such a capability could be achieved by IS/Daesh, the benefits are clear. It would allow for both new social media content generation and the broadcasting of that content by computer algorithms alone. This would provide IS/Daesh an additional social media multiplier to enhance its propaganda, recruitment, and related activities. A case in point would be the automated generation of variants of the online IS/Daesh *Dabiq* magazine series with additional 'open-source Jihad' and the bomb making and active shooter TTPs (tactics, techniques, and procedures) to conduct it [16].

However, given how despised and hated IS/Daesh State is, none of the cutting-edge business ventures which posses this technology would ever have anything to do with it via direct contract or licensing services. The same, of course, can't be said for mercenary hackers, various organized crime groups, and pariah states such as North Korea which might see value in such a technology transfer based on a wild card scenario whose potentials we at least need to be cognizant of.

International Community Response Implications

Three levels of international response are being directed against IS/Daesh social media capabilities—that is, via major social media technology companies, cyber vigilante groups, and sovereign states. This response is being focused on both the human component of social media—human participants—and also on the bot and apps utilization and manipulation of that media. At its most basic level, companies like Twitter are closing IS/Daesh associated accounts, terminating the use of specific apps, and attempting to eliminate bot farms.

In turn, vigilante groups such as Anonymous have released "IS @" listings on Twitter and other entities—such as Japanese hacktivists—have utilized this information and begun bombarding them with anime and other forms of ridicule [17]. IS/Daesh affiliated accounts on other media platforms such as Facebook, Instagram, and Snapchat are also being targeted. Due to the sophistication of many of these cyber vigilantes and hacktivists, an army of anti-IS/Daesh bots have increasingly been created to combat its member and affiliate social media activities. In such a 'bot on bot war,' the IS/Daesh is presently now on the defensive.

Finally, many sovereign Arab states in the Middle East are currently engaging in counter IS/Daesh social media [18]. If any of these states have the capacity to drawn upon esoteric systems such as the shadowy "Social Networking Influence Engine" is unknown—though, if this were the case, it would likely be Saudi Arabia initially. This may not be so far fetched given that the Syrian government as early as 2011 utilized Twitter bot nets that automatically intimidated social media protestors as part of a psychological warfare campaign [19].

The Social Networking Influence Engine is likely far more advanced and artificial intelligence based. It could thus be programmed to launch automated text counter-narratives which it creates and then direct them back at social media posts and accounts exhibiting pro-IS/Daesh related sentiment [20]. We must also not forget that America also has its own cyber-influence capabilities and may have already begun or may be on the verge of unleashing its own second phase automated social media barrage against that terrorist entity.

In summation, bots, apps, and automated text generators represent some of the forms of the 'cyber weapons' being utilized in the social media conflict between IS/Daesh and the international community. In such a changing conflict landscape, victory is increasingly computer science and artificial intelligence driven. In this emerging arena, that terrorist organization now appears to be more and more at a disadvantage.

Notes

[1] Jim Michaels, "Islamic State recruiting offsets 15,000 killed by airstrikes in past year." *USA Today.* 29 July 2015, http://www.usatoday.com/story/news/world/2015/07/29/air-campaign-kills-15000-isis-militants-pentagon-iraq-syria/30750327/.

[2] For this Arabic tweet stream see https://twitter.com/activehashtags. J. M. Berger, "How ISIS Games Twitter." *The Atlantic.* 16 June 2014, http://www.theatlantic.com/international/archive/2014/06/isis-iraq-twitter-social-media-strategy/372856/.

[3] Part of this shift can be attributed to counter-information campaigns waged by Arab states—especially from Saudi Arabia and Egypt—against IS. See "Explosive Growth in ISIS Tweets: Arabic Overtakes English." *Recorded Future.* 25 February 2015, https://www.recordedfuture.com/isis-twitter-growth/.

[4] Mami Maruko, "Malware targets users seeking info on Islamic State group." *The Japan Times News.* 4 February 2015, http://www.japantimes.co.jp/news/2015/02/04/national/crime-legal/malware-targets-users-seeking-info-islamic-state-group/.

[5] Victoria Woollaston, "Rise of the Twitter bots: Social network admits 23 MILLION of its users tweet automatically without human input." *Daily Mail.* 13 August 2014, http://www.dailymail.co.uk/sciencetech/article-2722677/

Rise-Twitter-bots-Social-network-admits-23-MILLION-users-tweet-automatically-without-human-input.html.

[6] INSS-CSFI, "USA—Bots are great weapon for cyber terrorist." *Executive Cyber Intelligence Report.* 1 December 2014, http://www.tripwire.com/state-of-security/government/executive-cyber-intelligence-report-december-1-2014/.

[7] Rebecca Grant, "Facebook has no idea how many fake accounts it has — but it could be nearly 140M." *Venture Beat.* 3 February 2014, http://venturebeat.com/2014/02/03/facebook-has-no-idea-how-many-fake-accounts-it-has-but-it-could-nearly-140m/, James Parsons, "Facebook's War Continues Against Fake Profiles and Bots." *Huffington Post.* 22 May 2015, http://www.huffingtonpost.com/james-parsons/facebooks-war-continues-against-fake-profiles-and-bots_b_6914282.html, and "Number of monthly active Facebook users worldwide as of 2nd quarter 2015 (in millions)." *Statista.* Nd, http://www.statista.com/statistics/264810/number-of-monthly-active-facebook-users-worldwide/ (Accessed 30 July 2015).

[8] For more on this topic see Steven Levy, "Can an Algorithm Write a Better News Story Than a Human Reporter." *Wired.* April 2012, http://www.wired.com/2012/04/can-an-algorithm-write-a-better-news-story-than-a-human-reporter/, Gini Graham Scott, "Assault on Writers From Automated Software." *Huffington Post.* 29 May 2013, http://www.huffingtonpost.com/gini-graham-scott/automated-writing-technology_b_2974756.html, Ross McGuinness, "Meet the robots writing your news articles: The rise of automated journalism." *Metro.* 10 July 2014, http://metro.co.uk/2014/07/10/meet-the-robots-writing-your-news-articles-the-rise-of-automated-journalism-4792284/, and Klint Finley, "In the Future, Robots Will Write News

That's All About You." *Wired*. March 2015, http://www.wired.com/2015/03/future-news-robots-writing-audiences-one/.

[9] David J. Hill, "Patented Book Writing System Creates, Sells Hundreds of Thousands of Books On Amazon." *SingularityHUB*. 13 December 2012, http://singularityhub.com/2012/12/13/patented-book-writing-system-lets-one-professor-create-hundreds-of-thousands-of-amazon-books-and-counting/. For a present listing of 687,306 results for Icon Group International books on Amazon see http://www.amazon.com/s?ie=UTF8&page=1&rh=n%3A283155%2Cp_27%3AIcon%20Group%20International.

[10] David J. Hill, "Patented Book Writing System Creates, Sells Hundreds of Thousands of Books On Amazon."

[11] Richard Moss, "Creative AI: Teaching computers to be reporters and storytellers." *Gizmag*. 9 February 2015, http://www.gizmag.com/creative-ai-automated-writing-storytelling/35989/.

[12] Bob Crilly, "How ISIS jihadists spread hate with Twitter army of 45,000." *The Telegraph*. 28 January 2015, http://www.telegraph.co.uk/news/worldnews/islamic-state/11373519/How-Isil-jihadists-spread-hate-with-Twitter-army-of-45000.html.

[13] J. M. Berger and Jonathon Morgan, *The ISIS Twitter Census: Defining and describing the population of ISIS supporters on Twitter*. Analysis Paper No. 20. Washington, DC: The Brookings Institute. March 2015: 25, http://www.brookings.edu/~/media/research/files/papers/2015/03/isis-twitter-census-berger-morgan/isis_twitter_census_berger_morgan.pdf/.

[14] Ibid: 25, 28.

[15] David J. Hill, "Patented Book Writing System Creates, Sells Hundreds of Thousands of Books On Amazon."

[16] "The Islamic State's (ISIS, ISIL) Magazine." *The Clarion Project.* 10 September 2014, http://www.clarionproject.org/news/islamic-state-isis-isil-propaganda-magazine-dabiq. For information on the earlier and ongoing Al Qaida *Inspire* series see Anthony F. Lemieux, "*Inspire* Magazine: A Critical Analysis of its Significance and Potential Impact Through the Lens of Information, Motivation, and Behavioral Skills Model." *Terrorism and Political Violence.* Vol. 26., 2014: 354-371.

[17] See "ISIS email,websites and ip's exposed by @CosmoSQL #GhostSec." *Pastebin.* 19 July 2015, http://pastebin.com/dYQx0Rd9 and Ollie McAteer, "How Japanese anime is the latest weapon in the fight against Isis." *Metro.* 23 July 2015, http://metro.co.uk/2015/07/23/how-japanese-anime-is-the-latest-weapon-in-the-fight-against-isis-5309562/.

[18] For example, the UAE and USA governments recently announced the launch of the Sawab Center, http://www.sawabcenter.org/. According to the website the organization has been created "in order to counter DAESH propaganda and reveal its true criminal nature and intent."

[19] INSS-CSFI, "USA—Bots are great weapon for cyber terrorist." *Executive Cyber Intelligence Report.* See originally Anas Qtiesh, "Spam Bots Flooding Twitter to Drown Info About #Syria Protests [Updated]." *Global Voices Advocacy.* 18 April 2011, http://advocacy.globalvoicesonline.org/2011/04/18/spam-bots-flooding-twitter-to-drown-info-about-syria-protests/. Another basic counter-narrative bot example, in this instance related to climate change—whose account has since been closed

by Twitter—is as follows: "Leck's bot, @AI_ AGW, doesn't just respond to arguments directed at Leck himself, it goes out and picks fights. Every five minutes it trawls Twitter for terms and phrases that commonly crop up in Tweets that refute human-caused climate change. It then searches its database of hundreds to find a counter-argument best suited for that tweet —usually a quick statement and a link to a scientific source." See "Artificial Trolls in GD." *AR15.COM*. 25 March 2015, http://www.ar15. com/archive/topic.html?b=1&f=5&t=1731426.

[20] Joel Harding, "Is Information Really a Weapon?" *To Inform Is To Influence*. 12 December 2014, http://toinformistoinfluence. com/2014/12/12/is-information-really-a-weapon/.

Further Readings

David J. Hill, "Patented Book Writing System Creates, Sells Hundreds of Thousands of Books On Amazon." *SingularityHUB*. 13 December 2012, http://singularityhub. com/2012/12/13/patented-book-writing-system-lets-one-professor-create-hundreds-of-thousands-of-amazon-books-and-counting/.

Steven Levy, "Can an Algorithm Write a Better News Story Than a Human Reporter." *Wired*. April 2012, http://www. wired.com/2012/04/can-an-algorithm-write-a-better-news-story-than-a-human-reporter/.

P. W. Singer and Emerson T. Brooking, *LikeWar: The Weaponization of Social Media*. Boston, MA: Houghton Mifflin Harcourt, 2018: 1-416.

Essay 8

Daesh/IS Armored Vehicle Borne Improvised Explosive Devices (AVBIEDs)—Insurgent Use and Terrorism Potentials

This essay in the Terrorism Futures series focuses on advanced threats related to vehicle borne improvised explosive devices (VBIEDs). It provides a threat typology of these devices with their evolution into the armored (AVBIED) variant that has now been fielded by Daesh/IS in both Iraq and Syria. A short overview of such insurgent use will be provided as well as a brief discussion of the terrorism potentials of such use if directed against the UAE, Europe, or the United States.

VBIED Threat Typology

Vehicle borne improvised explosive devices (VBIEDs), or simply vehicle bombs, have existed since the September 1920 deployment of 'Buda's Wagon'—an actual horse drawn wagon filled with explosives and scrap metal—at Wall and Broad streets in downtown Manhattan by the anarchist Mario Buda. The attack left 40 dead and over 200 injured and, at the time, prompted a national emergency in the US [1].

This iteration of these weapons—dominated by car, van, and truck platforms—can be considered Type 1 devices in the sense that they represent both a static and unarmored form of VBIED. Not normally associated with suicide (or martyrdom) operations, because the driver does not have to remain with the vehicle upon detonation, these devices have been used extensively throughout the world, especially in the West. One concentration of such car bombings took place in both Northern Ireland and in England from the 1970s through the 1990s. They were carried out by the Irish Republication Army (IRA) in coordination with other forms of attacks utilizing thrown and emplaced bombs, improvised mortars, incendiaries, and small arms. In the United States, the first World Trade Towers Bombing in 1993 and the Oklahoma City Bombing that took place a few years later are additional examples of the use of Type 1 VBIEDs. Multiple devices (e.g., secondary devices) are typically utilized in a time delay mode which seeks to inflict casualties to responding forces by detonating in likely command post and triage areas adjacent to the initial bombing or along expected avenues of approach for emergency vehicles.

The next iteration of vehicular bombs—their Type 2 form—is derived from the *mobile* variant of these *unarmored* devices. Their initial use by Shia militias and later Hezbollah became publicized during the 1982 Israeli invasion of Southern Lebanon and ongoing Israeli operations through 1985 as well as against US and French troops in 1983. VBIEDs were driven into the middle of Israeli military convoys and then detonated—a major concern of US and allied forces in Iraq twenty years later when the initial insurgency broke out against the Multinational

Force (MNF) led by the U.S. Type 2 VBIEDs were also utilized against high value targets during the Lebanon conflict when one such device was deployed against the US Embassy in Beirut in April 1983, damaging the embassy building and killing 63 personnel, and another was utilized in the October 1983 against the Marine Barracks which leveled the building and killed 241 US servicemen [2].

An even more sophisticated VBIED employment incident took place in Grozny, Chechnya in December 2002, utilizing two vehicles working together in tandem. In this incident, perpetrated by Riyadus-Salikhin and directed against the Chechen state Headquarters, two vehicles—one purported to be driven by a 17-year old boy and the other driven by his father and 15-year old sister—were utilized sequentially, with the first running down the perimeter fences and the second one carrying the main explosive charge. The detonating 2nd VBIED destroyed the 4-story building and caused 72 deaths and over 200 injuries [3]. This operation, masterminded by Shamil Basayev—the infamous Islamist warlord and terrorist responsible for the 2004 Beslan school massacre—may very well be considered an early firebreak TTP (Tactics, Techniques, and Procedures) that later groups would conceptually draw upon for their own VBIED attacks against heavily fortified facilities [4].

The newest, or Type 3, VBIED iteration represents an advancement to the Type 2 form in that the device is now not only *mobile* but also *armored* in order to increase its survival probability of reaching the intended target. Terms for this armor application includes 'hillbilly' and 'Mad Max' armor as well as the designation 'heavy VBIED' [5]. These armored suicide bombing vehicles can be utilized individually or in groups against secure compounds and high value infrastructure and are far less vulnerable to defending fire than the earlier unarmored

Type 2 variant. Rather than simply a projected evolutional form of VBIED, these devices have now become a reality in insurgent operational environments in the Middle East.

Insurgency Use

The use of AVBIEDs—and improvised armor placed on cars, trucks, and construction equipment for armored fighting vehicle (AFV) purposes in general—in Iraq and Syria by Daesh/IS has been discussed in quite a few articles and news reports, beginning in late 2013 [6]. These vehicles run the gamut from civilian vehicles and commercial trucks through bulldozers and dump trucks into actual military vehicles such as captured armored HMMWVs (High Mobility Multipurpose Wheeled Vehicles) [7] and M113 APCs (Armored Personnel Carriers) [8].

The Daesh/IS has been utilizing AVBIEDs as a substitute for a lack of heavy artillery units and has directed their use against garrisoned bases and towns in Iraq and Syria during breeching assaults into them. Over the course of the last few years, AVBIED use has evolved to the point where they have not only been used individually and in small groups but *en masse*, with thirty such vehicles utilized during the capture of the Iraqi city of Ramadi in May 2015:

> In the first wave, the jihadis packed a bulldozer with explosives, which then successfully obliterated a security perimeter around an Iraqi government compound. Immediately after, about 30 vehicles flooded into the then-contested city, setting off another series of massive explosions, according to reports.

Ten of the thirty car bombs detonated resulted
in such massive explosions that they packed
enough comparable firepower to the 1995
Oklahoma City truck bomb, ABC News
reports [9].

This refined TTP—reminiscent of the earlier Riyadus-
Salikhin attack in Grozny—utilized an adhoc collection of
AVBIEDs including an armored bulldozer, at least one M113
APC, a number of armored HMMWVs, as well as vehicles
retrofitted with mprovised armor appliques [10]. The attack
resulted in entire blocks of Ramadi being obliterated and,
ultimately, the complete route of the defending Iraqi troops
from the city [11].

These 'Franken-trucks,' as some have labeled them, may
even be getting more potentially bizarre and high tech [12]. The
capture of the recent Daesh/IS "jihadi university video," which
contains information on a new driverless vehicle capability, may
well represent another evolving variant of future AVBIED use.
As an outcome of this new capability, a suicide (e.g. martyrdom)
driver is no longer required to drive the vehicle into the intended
target. Rather, a remote controlled steering, accelerating, and
braking system is utilized along with a mannequin rigged with
thermal output capability to mimic the heat signature given off
by a human driver [13]. The intent here is to 'spoof' security
service use of standoff thermal sensing equipment—that is, to
make it register that a human being is driving the vehicle—at
key avenues of approach and facility access control check points.

Terrorism Potentials

To date, concerns in the UAE, Europe, and the United
States have focused on unarmored VBIEDs. While an ongoing

and known threat capability exists concerning static car and truck bombs deployed at choke and channeling points, it is their mobile use in attacking secure governmental and other high value facilities that is of even greater concern. Various access control methods, ranging from serpentine roadways through mobile road spikes and barriers, exist that will slow down or stop a mobile VBIED attack. The follow-on response force protocol utilized in combination with such access control measures is deadly small arms fire directed at the terrorist personnel that are driving the threat vehicle as well as any supporting terrorist security forces.

The use of one or more armored VBIEDs drastically changes this defensive equation. In a minimum access control scenario, a vehicle bombing attack may be slowed down enough for friendly forces to engage the AVBIED but, given its probable ballistic protection levels, the effects of such deadly response (comprised of semi-auto pistol though light assault rifle fires) will now be negated. In such a scenario, the AVBIED has a much greater likelihood of reaching its intended detonation point than a normal VBIED would be able to achieve. In a second scenario in which high levels of access control measures exist, a singular IED carrying vehicle—even an armored one—would likely not breech the initial barrier system. In this second scenario, now, however two or more AVBIEDs can be deployed as has been witnessed in the many recent Daesh/IS AVBIED attacks in Syria and Iraq. The first AVBIED penetrates as deeply as it can into a facility's access control defense and then detonates in place in order to clear a path for the next AVBIED to reach the mission's intended detonation point [14].

Both of the above AVBIED scenarios suggest that, at a minimum, a reevaluation of both access control protocols and responding force armaments needs to be conducted. Such a reevaluation would determine if armored vehicles—such as executive SUVs (Sport Utility Vehicles) with ballistic armor kits or more improvised systems as utilized by Daesh/IS in Iraq and Syria—should be identified as a realistic threat to a specific facility and, as a result, if environmental design and response planning considerations—including a provision for the acquisition of greater penetrative weaponry such as 7.62 mm AP (Armor Piercing) or even .50 Cal M82CQ Carbine-like systems for driver compartment and engine block kill capability—should now be made.

Notes

[1] Mike Davis, *Buda's Wagon: A Brief History of the Car Bomb.* London: Verso, 2007: 1-3.

[2] For a short video chronicling this incident, see "Beirut Remembered – The Marine Barracks Terrorist Attack, 1983." *You Tube.* Posted 8 January 2014, https://www.youtube.com/watch?v=JvFRirhbn5M.

[3] Nick Paton Walsh, "Suicide family 'behind Grozny blast.'" *The Guardian.* 25 February 2003, http://www.theguardian.com/world/2003/feb/26/chechnya.nickpatonwalsh. The video of the actual attack taken by Chechen terrorists and posted online is reposted at this link: http://www.liveleak.com/view?i=669_1184182183&comments=1.

[4] Competing narratives include the fact that the terrorists were wearing uniforms, utilized military license plates, or had official passes to get into the facility. Some sort of security breakdown—including the possible bribing of gate guards—may also have taken place. See, for instance, Michael Wines,

"Suicide Bombers Kill at Least 46 At Chechen Government Offices." *The New York Times*. 28 December 2002, http://www.nytimes.com/2002/12/28/world/suicide-bombers-kill-at-least-46-at-chechen-government-offices.html and "Moscow points to Grozny's Arab tie." *CNN*. 29 December 2002, http://edition.cnn.com/2002/WORLD/europe/12/28/chechnya.toll/.

[5] "'Heavy' VBIED (Vehicles w/ Armor) in Syria." *Breach Bang Clear*. 21 December 2013, http://www.breachbangclear.com/mad-max-armor-vbied-in-syria/.

[6] See, for instance, "Growing Jihadi Use of Improvised Armor on VBIEDs, Technicals & Other Vehicles." *IntelCenter*. n.d., http://intelcenter.com/reports/jihadi-improvised-armor-trend/#gs.8zlTi4g and "Weapons: Can Your Defensive Plan Counter An Armored VBIED?" *Feral Jundi*. 21 December 2013, http://feraljundi.com/5952/weapons-can-your-defensive-plan- counter-an-armored-vbied/.

[7] David Francis, "The Islamic State Is Using Humvees as Suicide Bombs. The U.S. Is Sending More." *Foreign Policy*. 5 June 2015, http://foreignpolicy.com/2015/06/05/the-islamic-state-is-using-humvees-as-suicide-bombs-the-u-s-is-sending-more/.

[8] Mike Hoffman, "ISIS Releases Photos of Militants Using U.S. M113s as VBIEDS." *DefenseTech*. 30 October 2014, http://defensetech.org/2014/10/30/isis-releases-photos-of-militants-using-u-s-m113s-as-vbieds/.

[9] Jordan Schactel, "ISIS Suicide Truck Bombs Took Out 'Entire City Blocks' During Ramadi Raid." *Breitbart*. 21 May 2015, http://www.breitbart.com/national-security/2015/05/21/

isis-suicide-truck-bombs-took-out-entire-city-blocks-during-ramadi-raid/.

[10] Sean D. Naylor, "The Islamic State's Best Weapon Was Born in the USA." *Foreign Policy*. 4 June 2015, http://foreignpolicy.com/2015/06/04/hell-on-wheels/.

[11] The note refers to the *Armored HMMWV with Welded Ram/Plating and Rear Plating Used as VBIED. Utilized Against Shia Military Base in Western Iraq in October 2015 Islamic State Social Media [For Public Distribution]* now found in the image gallery of the book. For more on this incident, see Bill Gertz, "Islamic State Used Captured Humvee in Suicide Bombing." *The Washington Free Beacon*. 4 November 2015, https://freebeacon.com/national-security/islamic-state-used-captured-humvee-in-suicide-bombing/. The AVBIED video frame image used in this essay was independently taken from the original Islamic State social media posting and not from the Gertz article.

[12] Trent Baker, "Islamic State Suicide Bombers Unleashing 'Franken-Truck' on Kurds: 'Something Out of a Movie.'" *Breitbart*. 22 November 2015, http://www.breitbart.com/video/2015/11/22/islamic-state-suicide-bombers-unleashing-franken-truck-on-kurds-something-out-of-a-movie/.

[13] Stuart Ramsay, "Exclusive: Inside IS Terror Weapons Lab." *Sky News*. 6 January 2016, http://news.sky.com/story/1617197/exclusive-inside-is-terror-weapons-lab.

[14] Road cratering issues for second vehicle follow-on exist but can be mitigated via TTP and technology use protocols.

Further Readings

Mike Davis, *Buda's Wagon: A Brief History of the Car Bomb*. London: Verso, 2007: 1-228.

David Hambling, "Why ISIS Is Building Mad Max Truck Bombs." *Popular Mechanics*. 23 February 2016, https://www.popularmechanics.com/military/weapons/news/a19555/why-isis-is-building-mad-max-truck-bombs/.

Hugo Kaaman, "The History and Adaptability of the Islamic State Car Bomb." 14 February 2017, https://hugokaaman.com/2017/02/14/the-history-and-adaptability-of-the-islamic-state-car-bomb/.

Essay 9

Laptop Bombs and Civil Aviation—Terrorism Potentials and Carry-On Travel Bans

This insight in the Terrorism Futures series focuses on the heightened concerns expressed over the smuggling of explosives hidden in laptops by Al Qaeda, and now Islamic State/Daesh, operatives for civil aviation bombing purposes. It will provide an overview of ongoing radical Islamist airliner explosive device targeting approaches and activities, a red team analysis of the terrorism potentials related to the laptop bombing mode of attack, and a short discussion of the laptop (as well as similar sized electronic device) travel bans that have been enacted and are now being considered.

Civil Aviation Bombings

Passenger airliners have been the targets of terrorist bombing attacks for some decades now with Gulf Air Flight 771 crashing into the desert near Abu Dhabi, UAE in September 1983, Air India Flight 182 breaking up after taking off from Montreal,

Canada in June 1985, and Pan Am Flight 103 exploding over Lockerbie, Scotland in December 1988 representing some of the earliest and most catastrophic incidents.

While various terrorist groups have engaged or attempted to engage in these forms of attacks, since the mid-1990s Al Qaeda has made a concerted effort to target airliners. This concerted effort is composed of nine incidents directly linked to that organization along with one incident indirectly linked (via Shamil Basayev's Chechen group). In addition, a relatively recent incident in October 2015 conducted by Daesh has also taken place. These civil aviation explosive device targeting incidents have been undertaken via one of four approaches: checked baggage (or parcel cargo), close to the body, internal body (animal), or carry on item devices—which have been alternatively utilized over time in an attempt to bypass airport screening technologies and protocols [1].

The final approach—based on using carry-on items to hide the bomb—is a predominant one and has taken place in five incidents found in December 1994, January 1995, August 2006, October 2015, and February 2016. The initial three were all liquid explosive based—the first two of which [2] were components of Ramzi Yousef's Bojinka plot and the later one [3] an Al Qaeda London cell plot. This TTP (Tactic, Technique, and Procedure) has been subsequently neutralized by carry on liquid bans (over a certain amount) and new liquid explosive detection capabilities. The fourth incident—the Russian Metrojet Flight bombing in October 2015 out of Sharm El Sheikh is still shrouded in mystery. It may have involved an explosive placed in a beverage can, but it would have required the Daesh operative to manually toggle the device which would not normally be possible since such a beverage can should not have been allowed through airport security [4]. The fifth carry-on items incident targeted

Daallo Airlines Flight 159 out of Mogadishu to Djibouti City. In this incident, Abdullahi Abdisalam Borleh, an Al Shabab operative with likely AQAP technical support, detonated a laptop bomb that resulted in a hull breach that killed him and injured two nearby passengers. The aircraft had not reached cruising altitude which likely saved it from destruction and it was able to safely make an emergency landing [5].

It is this approach utilizing a laptop bomb in February 2016, along with earlier 2014 intelligence relating to AQAP bomb making TTPs [6] shared with the Al Qaeda 'Khorasan' component in Syria and finally now unspecified Daesh heightened interest [7] in civil aviation bombings, that has triggered the recent laptop and similar sized electronic devices travel bans on certain international flights.

Terrorism Potentials

The major technical decision points, related to smuggling laptop bombs onto passenger airlines, pertains to bypassing contemporary airport screening measures in the areas of *explosives detection* and *laptop forensics and functionality tests*. Soft considerations also exist. They include smuggling bomb laden laptops through lower tier airports with inadequate screening technologies, procedures, and practices and using confederates that share the attacker's ideology or are simply paid off (e.g. the insider threat) to help allow the laptop through security and onto the targeted airliner [8].

Explosives detection defeat strategies can be focused on either utilizing new and novel forms of explosives that are not in scanner datasets, or utilizing known threat explosives that have had their residue and off-gassing signatures masked so that common swabbing/patching and machine olfaction techniques are neutralized. For terrorist mission requirements, explosive signature masking and/or elimination is preferable as it relies upon the utilization of known and effective explosives rather than attempting to develop new and unproven ones outside of known explosive chemical groupings presently being screened for. Such signature masking and elimination can be attempted to be accomplished by means of clean room-like techniques and the vacuum sealing of explosives, or by using non-porous device skin materials, with acetone and alcohol baths to mask explosive signatures in bomb designs.

Laptop forensics and functionality test defeat focuses on making sure that x-ray imaging (and potentially decay signature sensing) of a laptop will not result in anomaly detection related to its internal components and, if a laptop is turned on, that it will minimally function during an inspection. The intent is to facilitate a 'contextual narrative' for the device that airport screeners will accept and thus allow it to pass through their screening procedures. To effectively bypass the x-ray screening hurdle, a terrorist group would be required to take baseline images of a laptop to provide a comparative standard against IED (Improvised Explosive Device) alterations required to turn the computer artifact into a functioning bomb. Laptop selection criteria would be based on ubiquitous business systems that have reasonable cost so as not to stand out while at the same time possess relative bulkiness so that enough internal space exists for alterations to be made without making the laptops non-functioning. Explosive caching focal points would be internal optical drives, though most newer laptops no longer come with them, hard drives, batteries, and void spaces that can be made to appear as functioning components as well as external USB optical drives and other peripherals. The laptop bomb alterations need to be done in such a way that, if a screener asks for the system to be turned on, it must appear to minimally function.

While such airport screening defeat strategies may represent major obstacles for terrorist groups, Al Qaeda affiliates appear to be making progress with their homebrew lab capabilities. More of a concern is the ability of Daesh, until recently, to command more technical resources than any other previous terrorist organization in existence. That entity has possessed the scientific capacity of a city-state with its over two-year control of the University of Mosul, one of the largest research centers in the Middle East, as well as satellite, universities in Raqqa, Deir Ezzor, and al-Hassaka Syria. At a minimum, we know that various university facilities in Mosul, as well as in Raqqa, were put on a war footing and used to research and produce weaponry for Daesh [9].

Additionally, Daesh has had access to airport screening equipment captured from Mosul International Airport (OSM) and potentially from some smaller airports within their earlier territorial footprint in Iraq and Syria. The Mosul airport security equipment manifest is unclear, with an unknown potential number of x-ray machines, metal detectors and/or explosive residue sensors that may have been seized from it's sole passenger terminal. As of June 2003, a Heimann Hi-Scann 6040TS screening system (if functioning is unknown) was evident in the departures area but there was "no walk-thru detecting equipment" existing at that time [10]. Later information on the airport's passenger screening capacity is not readily available so what actual screening machinery was seized is unknown. Still, given such a past technical capacity and possible access to some airport screening equipment, the potentials for the increased threat of laptop and related electronic device bombings of civil aviation have now undoubtedly increased.

These developments go a long way to help explain the proactive laptop and electronic device carry on bans enacted and being considered. Such bans are more typically reactive in nature and immediately implemented only after a specific airliner incident related to them has taken place. This logic pertains to the fact that such a long lag time exists from when the initial Al Qaeda Daallo Airlines Flight 159 laptop bombing took place in February 2016. The timing of the present carry on laptop and electronic device travel ban is thus very unusual coming over a year later and thus likely reflects the fact Daesh also now represents a credible laptop bombing threat to civil aviation.

Carry-On Laptop and Electronics Travel Bans

The present laptop (as well as similar sized electronic device) travel ban was enacted on 21 March 2017 by the U.S. Department of Homeland Security (DHS) [11]. It focuses on items commonly called "large electronic devices", including devices such as laptops, e-readers, cameras, and anything larger than a typical smartphone. The current ban focuses on aircraft departing from specific airports, on non-stop flights to the USA. Ten international airports are covered, from eight Middle Eastern and North African countries; Egypt, Jordan, Kuwait, Morocco, Qatar, Saudi Arabia, Turkey, and the United Arab Emirates. These airports are geographically clustered in the primary Daesh areas of regional operation in Iraq, Syria, and Libya. Additionally, AQAP (Al Qaeda in the Arabian Peninsula) and Al Qaeda Khorasan group elements in Syria and Iraq also possess operational capacity potentials in many of the nations that contain these airports. Of additional note is the fact that "There is no impact on domestic flights in the United States or flights departing the United States. Electronic devices will continue to be allowed on all flights originating in the United States" [12]

The United Kingdom simultaneously followed suit on 21 March 2017 with a similar laptop and electronic device cabin ban from last point of departure airports in Egypt, Jordan, Lebanon, Tunisia, Turkey, and Saudi Arabia [13]. Banned carry on laptops and electronic devices will be allowed in passenger luggage in airliner cargo bays under both the U.S. and UK new travel protocols, reflecting how much more difficult it is to detonate such IED devices by means of a timer, barometric, GPS, or remote texting initiator as opposed to by those devices carried into the cabin by a terrorist operative [14]. Of note is the fact that Western European nations, such as France and Germany, who are actively being targeted for attack by radical Islamists have not acceded to similar computer device travel bans.

Speculation persists that the laptop and electronic device ban may be expanded by DHS to cover additional specific last point of departure airports into the United States or become a blanket ban affecting all flights into the U.S. or even potentially be mandated for all international flights originating from the U.S. and/or domestic U.S. flights themselves [15]. One recent plan now mentioned may extend the ban from the present 10 international last point of departure airports to as many as 71 of them [16]. Such future determinations are still an unknown but will be based on some sort of cost-benefit analysis related to these increased safety requirements. These will be made in the face of actual incidents, plots, and intelligence related to Al Qaeda affiliate and Daesh activity versus lost business productivity for airline passengers and general security screening line slowdowns as well as revenue losses from a) less monies received from passenger inflight laptop and electronic device internet and movie purchases and b) future flight cancellations from business class and other passengers due to these travel carry on restrictions. Given the secretive nature of the intelligence warnings that have promoted the recent and ongoing laptop and electronic device bans, no determination can be presently made of its efficacy. What is known, however, is that radical Islamist terrorist groups are actively targeting civil aviation and the question regarding the next attack will not be a matter of if, but of when.

Notes

[1] The internal body cavity method using secreted bombs in humans has been utilized for VIP (Very Important Person) assassination attempts but not for airliner bombing purposes as of yet. See Robert J. Bunker and Christopher Flaherty (Primary Authors), *Body Cavity Bombers: The New Martyrs—A Terrorism Research Center Book*. Bloomington: iUniverse, 2013.

[2] Raymond Bonner and Benjamin Weiser, "Echoes of Early Design to Use Chemicals to Blow Up Airliners." *The New York Times*. 11 August 2006, https://www.nytimes.com/2006/08/11/world/europe/11manila.html?_r=0.

[3] Nic Robertson, Paul Cruickshank and Tim Lister, "Document shows origins of 2006 plot for liquid bombs on planes." *CNN*. 30 April 2012, https://www.cnn.com/2012/04/30/world/al-qaeda-documents/index.html.

[4] C. J. Chivers, "Bomb Experts Analyze the ISIS Soda-Can Bomb Photo." *The New York Times*. 18 November 2015, https://www.nytimes.com/live/paris-attacks-live-updates/a/.

[5] Robyn Kriel and Paul Cruickshank, "Source: 'Sophisticated' laptop bomb on Somali plane got through X-ray machine."

CNN. 12 February 2016, https://www.cnn.com/2016/02/11/africa/somalia-plane-bomb/index.html.

[6] Robert Liscouski and William McGann, "The Evolving Challenges for Explosive Detection in the Aviation Sector and Beyond." *CTC Sentinel*. Vol. 9, Iss. 5, May 2016: 1-6, https://www.ctc.usma.edu/the-evolving-challenges-for-explosive-detection-in-the-aviation-sector-and-beyond/.

[7] Pierre Thomas and Mike Levine, "New airplane electronics rules stem from ISIS-associated threat." *ABC News*. 21 March 2017, https://abcnews.go.com/Politics/airplane-electronics-rules-stem-isis-threat/story?id=46287186.

[8] Robert Liscouski and William McGann, "The Evolving Challenges for Explosive Detection in the Aviation Sector and Beyond."

[9] Stuart Ramsay, "Exclusive: Inside IS Terror Weapons Lab." *Sky News*. 5 January 2016, https://news.sky.com/story/exclusive-inside-is-terror-weapons-lab-10333883.

[10] *Aerodrome Assessment: Mosul Airport, Iraq*. SkyLink. June 2003, https://pdf.usaid.gov/pdf_docs/Pnacy265.pdf.

[11] Office of Public Affairs, *Fact Sheet: Aviation Security Enhancements for Select Last Point of Departure Airports with Commercial Flights to the United States (Updated July 21, 2017)*. Washington, DC: Department of Homeland Security. 21 July 2017, https://www.dhs.gov/news/2017/03/21/fact-sheet-aviation-security-enhancements-select-last-point-departure-airports.

[12] Ibid.

[13] *Hand luggage restrictions at UK airports*. London: Government of the United Kingdom, 21 March 2017, https://www.gov.uk/hand-luggage-restrictions/electronic-devices-and-electrical-items.

[14] Robert Wall and Susan Carey, "Broader Laptop Ban on Airplanes May Pose Fire Risk." *The Wall Street Journal*. 1 June 2017, https://www.wsj.com/articles/broader-laptop-ban-on-airplanes-may-pose-fire-risk-1496343634.

[15] David Schaper, "Fears Grow As DHS Officials Consider Expanding Airline Laptop Ban." *NPR*. 3 June 2017, https://www.npr.org/2017/06/03/531347271/fears-grow-as-dhs-officials-consider-expanding-airline-laptop-ban.

[16] Reuters, "Homeland Security: US Might Expand Laptop Ban to 71 Airports." *The Epoch Times*. 7 June 2017 (Updated 11 June 2017), https://www.theepochtimes.com/homeland-security-us-might-expand-laptop-ban-to-71-airports_2255692.html?utm_source=dlvr.it&utm_medium=twitter.

Further Readings

Robert J. Bunker, *Laptop Bombs and Civil Aviation Terrorism Potentials and Carry On Travel Bans*. TRENDS Working Paper 03/2017. 3 July 2017: 1-16, http://trendsresearch.org/research/laptop-bombs-and-civil-aviation-terrorism-potentials-and-carry-on-travel-bans/.

Robert J. Bunker, "Can Terrorists Beat the U.S. Laptop Ban, Screening Technologies?" *The Cipher Brief*. 12 July

2017, https://www.thecipherbrief.com/column_article/can-terrorists-beat-the-u-s-laptop-ban-screening-technologies.

Tom Cleary, "ISIS Laptop Bomb Threat: 5 Fast Facts You Need to Know." *Heavy*. 15 May 2017, https://heavy.com/news/2017/05/isis-laptop-bomb-threat-planes-carry-on-ban-europe-middle-east/.

Conclusion

Evolving Technology and TTPs Use

In the past, much of the concern about terrorist technology and TTPs (tactics, techniques, and procedures) proliferation has focused on CBRN (chemical, biological, radiological, and nuclear) usage—this mimicked concerns related to proliferation among pariah states shifting from conventional weaponry to those with indiscriminate mass killing potentials. While ISIS (Islamic State in Iraq and Syria) had at one point gained a bonified chemical warfare capability[1] and other terrorist groups have been involved in biological and radiological plots and sporadic incidents—and even have had nuclear aspirations—[2] their patterns of use have been more conventionally inspired, while at the same time, modified by low and high technology inclusion and/or by means of novel and creative TTPs application. Within the nine essays composing the core of the *Terrorism Futures* pocketbook, the technology and TTPs use themes highlighted are briefly summarized as follows:

- *Virtual Martyrdom:* The use of virtual reality (VR) for suicide drone, remote control IED cars and boats, and larger VBIED attacks in which the controller/driver is not killed in a martyrdom operation. They, in essence, become virtual martyrs and live to fight another day as in a video game in which players get more than one life with their characters and/or respawn. AS VR technologies and wireless communications improve, the ability to engage in such attacks increases. ISIS and other groups have in the past created remote controlled VBIEDs which could be utilized for such operations though the actual threat potentials due to ideology may be minimal [3]. *Impact:* None as of yet. VR CONOPS for terrorist attack purposes are still immature with martyrdom (self-sacrifice to god) viewed as the primary objective of Jihadi fighters who seek to enjoy the benefits and pleasures that paradise will provide them.

- *IED Drones:* The placement of an IED on a rotors or fixed wing unmanned aerial system (UAS)/unmanned aerial vehicle (UAV) which then detonates upon contact or in proximity of the target. *Impact:* A significant threat now exists with ISIS having used these weaponized devices extensively in Iraq and Syria before the territorial Caliphate was overrun. All major terrorist groups recognize the utility of IED drones and many—including Hezbollah (early pioneers of their use), Hamas, and Al Qaeda—have fielded them as have some Latin American criminal groups. In some instances, this form of drone usage has matured to dropping bomblet(s) that they now carry upon their intended targets, although this is presently more of an insurgent rather than a terrorist TTP.

- *Disruptive Targeting:* Terrorism is derived from bond-relationship rather than thing targeting. Terrorists do not have the destructive firepower to stand toe-to-toe with state security and military forces. It is not about the impact of the rock (akin to a physical terrorist attack) into the tranquil pond of society but rather the second order effects of the disruptive shock waves rippling across society's surface from the initial entry point. *Impact:* The disruptive targeting component of terrorist actions represents the basis of their targeting effects. This firepower basis is relatively well known within the terrorism research community but typically does not get well translated into 'societal bonds protection' by counterterrorism agencies and practitioners. Additionally, counter-narrative and counter-radicalization programs tend to be underdeveloped with a premium placed upon population, infrastructure, and force protection—that is, mitigating the physical effects of terrorist attacks rather than the disruptive ones.

- *Fifth Dimensional Battlespace:* Post-modern (advanced) battlespace is five-dimensional rather than four-dimensional in nature. It consists of a three-dimensional physical volume of space (x, y, z coordinate axis) existing in time (t)—traditional space-time—with the additional of a fifth-dimensional component that can warp space-time (c; cyber for informational effects and h; hyper for geometric effects). Terrorists engage in a conceptual cheat by not wearing military uniforms which allows them to achieve the defensive benefits that fifth-dimensional (non-targetable space) provides. *Impact:* The stealthing ability of terrorists to hide-in-plain-sight provides them with a defensive advantage that is still being utilized to this day. State policing, security, and military forces are continually attempting to overcome this defensive advantage by utilizing behavioral and data-mining systems as well as confidential informants (CIs) to identify terrorists residing within civilian populations.

- *Close to the Body Bombs:* IEDs placed on the human body for terrorism attack purposes have shifted for higher value and better protected targets from being overtly worn backpacks, vests, and belts to under the clothing devices which have then migrated to more intimate and less likely to be searched regions such as being taped to the torso, under the breasts (of women), in the groin area, or on the thighs or around the ankles, or even hidden under the soles of the feet (within the base or heels of shoes). The radical Islamist groups—primarily Sunni-extremist linked—have been the most innovative in this regard due to their willingness to engage in these forms of martyrdom operations. *Impact:* The aviation and related industries being targeted have been forced to continually upgrade their counterterrorism protocols and use of technology to mitigate these threats. These evolving devices represent a component of the ongoing multi-decade offensive-defensive dynamic of passenger airliner targeting and security countermeasures resultingly enacted.

- *Body Cavity Bombs:* The use of internal explosive devices placed in the human body (and also in animals such as dogs) represents a natural progression from the development and fielding of close to the body bombs. While such devices represent a tradeoff in payload and lethality effects (upon the intended target), they are far stealthier and harder to detect than externally placed suicide bombs if designed properly. To date, only Al

Qaeda and Taliban groups have fielded such devices for VIP and aircraft targeting purposes. *Impact:* The limited use of body cavity bombs has resulted in their being considered more of an exotic threat though some security focused groups, such as those tied to the European Union (EU), have been creating devices to scan for those and other internal body contraband (primarily illicit narcotics) [4]. These evolving devices represent a component of the ongoing multi-decade offensive-defensive dynamic of passenger airliner (and also VIP) targeting and security countermeasures then resultingly enacted.

- *Counter-Optical Lasers:* These systems range from weak red and green laser pointers, through commercial and hobby lasers into laser designators, and then onto dedicated military dazzle and blinding weapons. Higher energy lasers mounted on military vehicles, vessels, and aircraft also are now being fielded that can shoot down missiles, rockets, and drones. The lower energy counter-optical lasers can disrupt vision and also cause damage to the human eye which becomes a safety concern for the cockpit crew of passenger airliners. The Japanese Aum Shinrikyo cult (given the scientific training of many of its members) attempted to utilize lasers in the early 1990s, an insurgent group and a cartel have utilized them since, and some Jihadist groups have more recently expressed an interest in them. *Impact:* The fielding of these weapons systems by terrorists has been inconsequential to date yet is projected to eventually become more mainstream as these devices mature and younger generations of terrorists recognize their tactical and operational potentials.

- *Homemade Firearms:* The fabrication of homemade firearms—both crude ones made from scratch in village forges and back rooms from scrap metal and more sophisticated ones pieced together from unfinished yet machined and customized parts (aka Ghost Guns)—has been ongoing for many decades with regard to the crude ones and for many years with regard to the more sophisticated ones. Typically, semi-automatic assault rifles are converted into fully automatic ones, with their lower receivers swapped out with unfinished receivers (then finished) in the United States. Clandestine arms factories belonging to a cartel were raided in Mexico in November 2014 and were also part of the cottage industry utilized by the Islamic State in Syria and Iraq. *Impact:* Homemade firearms are far more likely to be utilized by right-wing extremists, militias, and terrorist groups (even if not designated as such) in the United States than in other regions. Weapons tracing issues related to many of these unregistered guns will exist and they can provide full-automatic firepower capability to their users, although in the hands of untrained (weekend warrior) shooters ammunition discipline and precision fires will be an issue.
- *Printed Firearms:* Between May 2013 and April 2015 a number of firearms and silencer variants were printed by 3D (additive) printers, first in hard plastics and then in metals with quite a number of downloadable printer files initially openly distributed on the internet and later embedded in secure Telegram channels. Criminals and drug dealers in some locales—such as Japan and Australia—became early adaptors to this new technology. Numerous new reports and articles have

since been written expressing terrorist use concerns. Such concerns partially bore fruit when, in October 2019, 3D printed lower receivers were seized from Kaleb Cole, a leader of the right-wing Atomwaffen Division. Cole was combining those receivers with metal gun parts to create automatic weapons, resulting in a hybrid form of homemade and printed weapon [5]. *Impact:* The use of printed firearms has been limited to date and more sensationalized than practical in their application by terrorist organizations. However, the low metal content of some of these firearms, the inability to trace them, and their print on demand availability in societies with strict gun laws and relatively few firearms circulating in society (such as in Japan and the UK) offer terrorist use potentials under certain operating scenarios. The ability to print metal silencers may, however, be even more significant from a traditional terrorist action perspective.

- *Remote Controlled Firearms:* This evolution in the use of firearms is derived from the hardline cable or wireless control of an assault rifle or other type of firearm by means of a game controller, smart phone, tablet, laptop, or desktop computer interface for targeting and C2 purposes. These systems have existed since the early 2000s with their battlefield usage beginning in the 2010s. The remote sniping, virtual targeting presence, and remote combined arms capabilities gained by these systems would have much practical utility for terrorist groups. *Impact:* These systems are being seen sporadically overseas such as in the Iraqi, Syrian, and Libyan conflict zones with their deployment by insurgent and terrorist groups. Higher end systems are also being developed by state military forces and even crowdsourced for Ukrainian military use (e.g. the Sabre Remote Weapon Station) [6]. Remote controlled firearms have not as of yet been utilized for terrorist attack purposes in Western societies. This is due to a moderate technical and CONOPS hurdle that underlies the lack of sophistication and creativity of most terrorist organizations and their members operating in the West.

- *Social Media Bots:* Botnets in this usage represent centrally controlled accounts in social media applications (e.g. Facebook, Twitter, and 4chan) that are linked to automated subaccounts (bots) that work together to spread a narrative for the user. In the case of terrorist organizations, botnets can be used for propaganda, recruitment, fundraising, and harassment (hate speech) purposes. *Impact:* The use of social media bots (and apps) and larger botnets has become increasingly common and utilized by private industry, political parties, non-governmental organizations (NGOs), extremists, and terrorists. While ISIS' 'Cyber Caliphate' is a shell of its former self, components of it are still operating and utilizing social media bots as are the remnant of its competitor Al Qaeda which is promoting its own narratives. Botnets were utilized in tandem with Hashtag Hijacking and specialized social media apps creation (The Dawn of Glad Tidings) by ISIS [7]. Right wing extremists and terrorist entities also have a large social media presence and utilize bots and botnets to get out their message of hate online—linked to Pepe the Frog and numerous other memes—across the internet.
- *AI Text Generators.* Artificial intelligence (AI) based text generators are increasingly approaching a level of

sophistication where they can convince humans that they are interacting with another human rather than an automated system. Such generators hold much promise for counter-narrative activities targeting ISIS, Al Qaeda, and other terrorist groups with a large online presence. *Impact*: To date, such text generators have been primarily beneficial to a few specialized book manufactures, news outlets, and online retail, social media, and marketing companies, as well as to authoritarian regimes for generating anti-US propaganda. Both terrorist groups—because of lack of sophistication—and liberal-democratic states—because of ethical inhibitions—appear to be behind in their utilization. Still, the danger that newer AI based systems such as the "GPT-2 text-generating language model" (via OpenAI) represent has been noted. In November 2019, it was said that GPT-2 "can be tweaked to generate synthetic propaganda to support white supremacy, Marxism, jihadist Islamism, and anarchism" [8].

- *AVBIEDs:* VBIEDs—parked and then later detonated (used early on by the IRA) or driven into their targets as a martyrdom operation (used by numerous radical Islamist groups)—have existed for decades now and are a well-known form of terrorist attack. The armoring of such weapons systems, turning them into armored vehicle borne improvised explosive devices (AVBIEDs), to allow them to better reach their intended targets in insurgent and conventional warfighting environments was pioneered by ISIS which utilized them in place of artillery for which they were deficient. *Impact:* While the potentials of armored VBIED usage have not been realized in Europe and the United States, when or if such deployment takes place will represent a significant security threat to hardened facilities and venues. Further, the TTP of a tandem attack in which the first AVBIED blows a hole in the defenses of a facility allowing the follow on one a clear path must also be considered in physical counterterrorism planning.

- *Laptop Bombs:* This theme focuses on the placement of explosives in computer laptops for aircraft targeting purposes. It represents a variant of the earlier use of turning desktop computers and/or their monitors into IEDs. The threat of these devices spiked in February 2016 with the Al Shabab (Al Qaeda linked) incident via a passenger airliner taking off from Mogadishu. Luckily, while the bomb detonated, the plane was not destroyed possibly because it had not as yet reached cruising altitude. *Impact:* The use of these explosive devices has resulted in increased physical screening procedures and computer functionality testing at domestic and international airports. These evolving devices represent a component of the ongoing multi-decade offensive-defensive dynamic of passenger airliner targeting and security countermeasures resultingly enacted.

Additionally, six candidate technologies and TTPs not discussed in the initial Terrorism Futures essays that have now been employed and/or offer potentials for their application by terrorist groups are as follows:

- *FPS/Live Streaming Attacks*: First person shooter (FPS) attacks later aired in online propaganda videos, and even lived streamed, allow terrorist groups to create a more immersive experience for their audiences. When live streamed, these have an almost addictive quality to them. Live streaming had been utilized by the knife welding ISIS linked terrorist Larossi Abballa in a FPS variant (first person stabber or slasher) incident on 13 June 2016 [9]. On 15 March 2019, white nationalist extremist Brenton Tarrant then live streamed his Christchurch shooting rampage on Facebook, showing its crossover appeal to a terrorist movement with far different ideological tenets than that adhered to by SOA [soldier(s) of Allah] [10]. *Impact:* Limited use to date although the technique has spread to a Mexican cartel—Cártel Santa Rosa de Lima (CSRL)—with a FPS incident (later uploaded to social media) taking place in Valle de Santiago, Guanajuato on 5 February 2019 [11].

- *Vehicular Overruns:* Since the 2010 Al Qaeda *Inspire* magazine issue containing the article "The ultimate mowing machine," low-tech vehicular overruns have been a component of Open Source Jihad (OSJ; Al Qaeda) and post-November 2016 Just Terror (JT; Islamic State) TTPs [12]. Ideal characteristics of the vehicles utilized for these attacks are "slightly raised chassis and bumper, fast in speed or rate of acceleration, double-wheeled load-bearing truck, large in size, and heavy in weight" [13]. These attacks can be stand-alone affairs though typically they are combined with the driver and one or more passengers engaging in a dismounted knife stabbing and slashing rampage or some other form of secondary attack once the overrun vehicle is rendered inoperable as in the case of the London Bridge attack in June 2017. *Impact:* The use of vehicular overruns has become a common Jihadist TTP in the United Kingdom, France, Germany, and other parts of the Western world. The TTP has, since June 2020, increasingly spread to protest (and, to a minor extent, civil unrest) incidents in the United States with far-right extremists engaging in what can be termed 'domestic terrorism' targeting protestors [14]. A future concern is the application of homemade armor or the stealing of an armored vehicle to engage in an overrun attack. This would give them and their driver more defensive protection which equates to better mission success. This trend has been seen with the transition from VBIEDs to AVBIEDs—though in Western societies creating such armor or stealing armored vehicles is far more problematic to undertake.

- *Mass Arson*: The use of arson attacks has been advocated in the Islamic State magazine *Rumiyah* (the January 2017 issue) and in the Al Qaeda magazine *Inspire* (the May 2012 and March 2013 issues) [15]. As evidenced by past Jihadist attacks, the arson component is generally auxiliary in nature, overly complex, and applied at the tactical level as part of a martyrdom action. The radical Islamist adherents engaging in these attacks are missing the larger operational and strategic implications of what can be accomplished utilizing them. Target sets such as "Apartment Buildings, Forests Adjacent to Residential Areas, and Factories," as advocated in *Rumiyah*, would result in large scale residential and urban fires and the potential for large death tolls and infrastructure devastation [16]. In May 2019, ISIS claimed to have used wildfires for crop destruction in various regions of Iraq and Syria as an insurgent tactic although this TTP has not been applied overseas for terrorism purposes [17]. *Impact:* While the origins of recent forest and brush fires in the American West, Australia, and other regions of the world are being closely monitored, links to terrorism have not been evident.

- *Collar Bombs*: These devices (aka 'necklace bombs') were utilized in by criminal organizations in Colombia for ransoming purposes in the early 2000s [18]. Their use has since sporadically spread globally for bank robbery and ransom purposes. Both live and hoax models have since been utilized. Variants include those made from hard plastic or galvanized tubing (containing the IED) fitted around the neck as well as a metal neck clamp and an attached metal box (containing the IED). Such devices are booby trapped and can possibly be command detonated. They pre-date geo-fencing TTP detonation CONOPS. The early Colombian and Venezuelan incidents were the May 2000 Elvia Cortez and June 2003 Jesus Orlando Guerrero events, respectively [19]. More geographically dispersed examples were the August 2003 Brian Douglas Wells ('pizza delivery man') incident in the US and August 2011 Madeleine Pulver incident in Australia [20]. Terrorist groups have not as yet recognized their use potentials. *Impact:* Presently, only a hypothetical—variant of securing a booby trapped or command detonated bomb vest or belt on an unwilling (or compromised—mentally challenged or drugged) participant in a suicide bomber terrorist attack.
- *HPM/RFW*: To date, high power microwave (HPM) and radio frequency weapons (RFWs)—whose biological and electronics effects can be utilized against humans as well as electronic equipment and infrastructure— have escaped the serious attention of most terrorist groups.

This is because these technologies are more advanced, unconventional in nature, and can be difficult to understand. Still, the recognition of their terrorism potentials in domestic counterterrorism planning has existed since the 1990s in the United States [21]. Present concerns relate to terrorists obtaining military grade HPM/RFW as well as creating their own improvised systems. The probable recent utilization of these systems against US diplomats by foreign state agents in 2016 and 2017 have further heightened fears that terrorists may recognize their operational utility [22]. Technology and TTPs use scenarios include attacking hospital equipment such as IVs for VIP assassination attempts, directly raising the brain temperatures of targeted individuals resulting in seizure and death, or taking down power generation infrastructure. *Impact:* This threat was typically only discussed in non-public counterterrorism planning meetings although increasing public awareness now exists.

- *Bio-Engineered Pathogens*: This technology harkens back to earlier CBRN use concerns but what has made the possibility of its utilization now far more likely is (a) advances in synthetic biology (SynBio) and DNA alteration which have greatly lowered the barrier to entry for malevolent groups engaging in biological terrorism and (b) the effects of COVID-19 which may represent an inspiration to some terrorist groups of what the weaponization of this technology offers.[23] The appeal of such attack scenarios will principally be to apocalyptic type cults and those organizations that believe that they can genetically target specific ethnic groupings in precision attacks. *Impact:* The effects of a bio-engineered pathogen being released and spreading globally could be catastrophic, potentially superseding the infection rates, death toll, economic loss, and disruption caused by the present COVID-19 pandemic.

In addition to the technology and TTPs discussed in the original Terrorism Futures essays and those identified in the above section, their use in everchanging combinations—along with more traditional forms of terrorism approaches (e.g. guns, bombs, and knives)—can be utilized for attack purposes. Akin to a military combined arms approach or the different warfare combinations advocated in the Chinese military work *Unrestricted Warfare*, this could be abstracted down to the primarily tactical level of terrorist group application [24]. Such layering can readily be seen in the use of a drone for ISR (intelligence, surveillance, and reconnaissance) which took place some months prior to Brenton Tarrant's March 2019 Christchurch FPS streaming rampage [25]. It must be ultimately remembered, however, that terrorist technology and TTPs use is a process undertaken in order to achieve disruptive targeting effects (via the generation of terror directed at a government and its population) by means of physically destructive actions and operations serving as a catalyst to achieve the higher order disruptive effects [26]. Hence, as this process becomes more sophisticated and deadly the expectation is that those disruptive effects will become more pronounced.

Notes

[1] Robert J. Bunker, *Contemporary Chemical Weapons Use in Syria and Iraq by the Assad Regime and the Islamic State.* Carlisle, PA: US Army War College, Strategic Studies Institute, February

2019, https://publications.armywarcollege.edu/publication-detail.cfm?publicationID=3676.

[2] See Peter Katona, Michael D. Intriligator, and John P. Sullivan, Eds., *Countering Terrorism and WMD: Creating a Global Counter-Terrorism Network*. London: Routledge, 2006: 1-328 and Brian Michael Jenkins, *Will Terrorists Go Nuclear?* Amherst, NY: Prometheus Books, 2008. Also see Brian Michael Jenkins, *Will Terrorists Go Nuclear?* P-5541. Santa Monica, RAND: 1975: 1-16, https://www.rand.org/pubs/papers/P5541.html.

[3] Hugo Kaaman, *The Myth of the Remote-Controlled Car Bomb*. European Eye on Radicalization. Report n.15, September 2019, https://eeradicalization.com/wp-content/uploads/2019/09/Hugo-Report-Remote-VBIEDs-Final.pdf.

[4] Robert J. Bunker, "EU MESMERISE Workshop: Internal (Body Cavity) & External (Stand Off Frisk) Contraband & Weaponry Scanning - 11-12 July 2019 - Alcalá de Henares, Spain." *Small Wars Journal*. 6 August 2019, https://smallwarsjournal.com/jrnl/art/eu-mesmerise-workshop-internal-body-cavity-external-stand-frisk-contraband-weaponry.

[5] Eric Woods, "Right-Wing Extremists' New Weapon." *Lawfare Blog*. 15 March 2020, https://www.lawfareblog.com/right-wing-extremists-new-weapon.

[6] "Sabre Remote Weapon Station." People's Project. com: Ukraine's military and civil crowdfunding. 20 February 2019, https://www.peoplesproject.com/en/sabre-remote-weapon-station/.

[7] Shane Shook, "Your Favorite Social Networks are Now Weapons of Terror." *Homeland Security Today.* 8 September 2014, https://www.hstoday.us/channels/global/your-favorite-social-networks-are-now-weapons-of-terror/.

[8] Liam Tung, "OpenAI's 'dangerous' AI text generator is out: People find GPT-2's words 'convincing.'" *ZDNet.* 6 November 2019, https://www.zdnet.com/article/openais-dangerous-ai-text-generator-is-out-people-find-gpt-2s-words-convincing/.

[9] Maura Conway & Joseph Dillon, *Case Study: Future Trends: Live-Streaming Terrorist Attacks?* VOX Pol, 2016, https://www.voxpol.eu/download/vox-pol_publication/Live-streaming_FINAL.pdf.

[10] Graham Macklin, "The Christchurch Attacks: Livestream Terror in the Viral Video Age." *CTC Sentinel.* Vol. 12, Iss. 6, July 2019, https://ctc.usma.edu/christchurch-attacks-livestream-terror-viral-video-age/.

[11] Robert J. Bunker, Alma Keshavarz and John P. Sullivan, "Mexican Cartel Tactical Note #39: GoPro Video Social Media Posting of Cártel Santa Rosa de Lima (CSRL) Tactical Action against Cártel Jalisco Nueva Generación (CJNG) in Guanajuato - Indications & Warning (I&W) Concerns." *Small Wars Journal.* 5 March 2019, https://smallwarsjournal.com/jrnl/art/mexican-cartel-tactical-note-39-gopro-video-social-media-posting-cartel-santa-rosa-de-lima.

[12] "Appendix 1. *Rumiyah* (Just Terror) and *Inspire* (Open Source Jihad) TTPs" in Robert J. Bunker and Pamela Ligouri Bunker, *The Islamic State English-Language Online Magazine Rumiyah* (Rome). Reston, VA: 100.

[13] Robert J. Bunker and Pamela Ligouri Bunker, *The Islamic State English-Language Online Magazine Rumiyah*: 61.

[14] Hannah Allam, "Vehicle Attacks Rise As Extremists Target Protesters." NPR. 21 June 2020, https://www.npr.org/2020/06/21/880963592/vehicle-attacks-rise-as-extremists-target-protesters?utm_medium=social&utm_campaign=npr&utm_source=twitter.com&utm_term=nprnews.

[15] See "Appendix 1. *Rumiyah* (Just Terror) and *Inspire* (Open Source Jihad) TTPs": 100 and Recognizing Arson with a Nexus to Terrorism." *First Responder's Toolbox*. 14 April 2017, https://www.dni.gov/files/NCTC/documents/jcat/firstresponderstoolbox/First Responders Toolbox-Recognizing Arson With a Nexus to Terrorism Originally Published-14 April 20171 May 2019-survey.pdf.

[16] "Appendix 1. *Rumiyah* (Just Terror) and *Inspire* (Open Source Jihad) TTPs": 61-62.

[17] "UN: Syrian fighters burning vital farmland is 'weapon of war.'" *Al Jazeera*. 4 June 2019, https://www.aljazeera.com/news/2019/06/04/un-syrian-fighters-burning-vital-farmland-is-weapon-of-war/ and Sebastian Murphy-Bates, "ISIS 'is using WILDFIRE as a terror weapon against its enemies'—with the group claiming responsibility for arson attacks that scorched land in Iraq and Syria and warning this is 'just the beginning.'" *Daily Mail*. 28 May 2019, https://www.dailymail.co.uk/news/article-7079723/ISIS-using-WILDFIRE-terror-weapon-against-enemies.html.

[18] These devices have also been said to have been used in Mexico and Israel. The term "terrorists" was generically used

in the article. See, Geoff Chambers, "Simple yet deadly device a favourite of overseas terrorists." *The Daily Telegraph*. 4 August 2011, https://www.dailytelegraph.com.au/news/nsw/simple-yet-deadly-device-a-favourite-of-overseas-terrorists/news-story/bdaedccf2fb3835028cecf28bd987862?sv=9504fb70d67efcc85c3e82c52c200b87.

[19] Scott Dalton, "Colombia Woman Killed by Neck Bomb." *AP News*. 15 May 2000, https://apnews.com/article/a93834c71e535b35f21459426035be42 and "Experts defuse necklace bomb." *BBC News*. 1 July 2003, http://news.bbc.co.uk/2/hi/americas/3036664.stm.

[20] Chris Summers, "Truth about US collar bomb robbery remains elusive." *BBC News*. 1 November 2020, https://www.bbc.com/news/world-us-canada-11098058 and Stephanie Holmes, "Unlacing the 'necklace bomb.'" *BBC News*. 4 August 2011, https://www.bbc.com/news/world-asia-pacific-14407161.

[21] For background on this threat, see Larry L. Altgilbers, Ian W. Merrit, and Howard Seguine, "Radio Frequency Weapons" in John P. Sullivan, Ed., *Jane's Unconventional Weapons Handbook*. Alexandria, VA: Jane's Information Group, 2000: 236-276 and Robert J. Bunker, "Radio Frequency Weapons: Issues and Potentials." *The Journal of California Law Enforcement*. Vol. 36, No. 1, 2002: 6-17.

[22] Eugene Poteat, "The Sound of Crickets: New dangers facing U.S. personnel serving abroad and possibly all of us." The Institute of World Politics. 30 April 2019, https://www.iwp.edu/articles/2019/04/30/the-sound-of-crickets-new-dangers-facing-u-s-personnel-serving-abroad-and-possibly-all-of-us/.

[23] Paul Cruickshank, "The most important national security question Trump and Biden need to address." *CNN*. 28 September 2020, https://www.cnn.com/2020/09/28/opinions/most-important-national-security-question-trump-biden-cruickshank/index.html. See also R. Daniel Bressler and Chris Bakerlee, "'Designer bugs': how the next pandemic might come from a lab." *Vox*. 6 December 2018, https://www.vox.com/future-perfect/2018/12/6/18127430/superbugs-biotech-pathogens-biorisk-pandemic. A variant of this technology is nano-tech based but this is generally viewed as beyond current terrorist organizational capacities to develop. See Louis A. Del Monte, *Nanoweapons: A Growing Threat to Humanity*. Lincoln, NB: Potomac Books, 2017.

[24] Matt Novak, "Terrorist Used Drone to Spy on Mosque Before Killing 51 People, Streaming Live on Facebook." *Gizmodo*. 26 August 2020, https://gizmodo.com/terrorist-used-drone-to-spy-on-mosque-before-killing-51-1844850596.

[25] Qiao Liang and Wang Xiangsui, *Unrestricted Warfare*. Beijing: PLA Literature and Arts Publishing House, February 1999. See the FBIS Translation, https://citeseerx.ist.psu.edu/viewdoc/summary?doi=10.1.1.169.7179.

[26] Even cyberterrorism has at its basis a destructive and compromising emphasis focusing on information and the ability to access that information. Certain disruptive forms of attack such as a denial-of-service (DoS) attack is conceptually no different than taking down a bridge span with a VBIED and denying choke point road access.

Additional Readings

The following additional readings provides the reader with a short listing of useful works pertaining to terrorist use of technology, terrorist TTPs, and terrorism futures. Special thanks to Rohan Gunaratna, Katalin Petho-Kiss, Rashmi Singh, Christopher Harmon, Brian Keith, David Ronfeldt, John Arquilla, and John P. Sullivan for their suggestions pertaining to these readings.

Robert J. Bunker and Pamela Ligouri Bunker, *The Islamic State English-Language Online Magazine Rumiyah (Rome).* Reston, VA: 2019: 59-62, 100-101 ('Just Terror' overview and complete 'Just Terror' and 'Open Source Jihad' reference listing).

Audrey Kurth Cronin, *Power to the People: How Open Technological Innovation is Arming Tomorrow's Terrorists.* New York, NY: Oxford University Press, 2019: 1-440.

Alan M. Dershowitz, *Why Terrorism Works: Understanding the Threat, Responding to the Challenge.* New Haven, CT: Yale University Press, 2003: 1-286.

Cynthia Dion-Schwarz, David Manheim, Patrick B. Johnston, *Terrorist Use of Cryptocurrencies*. RR-3026. Santa Monica, CA: RAND, 2019: 1-80.

Christopher Dobson and Ronald Payne, *The Terrorists: Their Weapons, Leaders, and Tactics*. New York, NY: Facts on File, 1982: 1-262.

Alan Dolnik, *Understanding Terrorist Innovation: Technology, Tactics and Global Trends*. Contemporary Terrorism Studies series. London, UK: Routledge, 2007: 1-220.

Richard English, *Does Terrorism Work? A History*. Oxford, UK: Oxford University Press, 2016: 1-350.

Daveed Gartenstein-Ross, Colin P. Clarke, and Matt Shear, "**Terrorists and Technological Innovation**." *Lawfare*. 2 February 2020.

John Giduck, *Terror at Beslan*. Golden, CO: Archangel Group, 2005: 1-392.

Seth Harrison, "**Evolving Tech, Evolving Terror**." New Perspectives in Foreign Policy, Issue 15, Spring 2018: 28-31.

Gregory D. Koblentz, "**Emerging Technologies and the Future of CBRN Terrorism**." *The Washington Quarterly*. Vol. 43, Iss. 2. 16 June 2020: 177-196.

Walter Laqueur and Christopher Wall, *The Future of Terrorism: ISIS, Al-Qaeda, and the Alt-Right.* New York, NY: Thomas Dunne Books, 2018: 1-272.

Michael K. Logan, Gina S. Ligon, and Douglas C. Derrick, "**Measuring Tactical Innovation in Terrorist Attacks**." *Journal of Creative Behavior*. 6 July 2019.

Rafat Mahmood and Michael Jetter, "**Communications Technology and Terrorism**." *The Journal of Conflict Resolution*. Vol. 64, Iss. 1, 1 January 2020: 127-166.

Malcolm W. Nance, ***Terrorist Recognition Handbook***. Boca Raton, FL: CRC Press, 2008: 1-480.

Evan Perkoski, "**Terrorist Technological Innovation**." Erica Chenoweth et al., Eds., *The Oxford Handbook of Terrorism*. Oxford, UK: Oxford University Press, 2019: 401-413.

H. John Poole, ***Tactics of the Crescent Moon: Militant Muslim Combat Methods***. Emerald Island, NC: Posterity Press, 2004: 1-360.

H. John Poole, ***Militant Tricks: Battlefield Ruses of the Islamic Insurgent***. Emerald Island, NC: Posterity Press, 2005: 1-412.

Magnus Ranstorp and Magnus Normark, Eds., ***Understanding Terrorism Innovation and Learning: Al-Qaeda and Beyond***. Political Violence series. London, UK: Routledge, 2015: 1-298.

Thomas Schelling, "**Thinking about Nuclear Terrorism**." *International Security*. Vol. 6, No. 4, Spring 1982: 61-77.

P. W. Singer and August Cole, ***Burn-In: A Novel of the Real Robotic Revolution***. New York, NY: Houghton Mifflin Harcourt, 2020: 1-432.

Stephen Sloan and Robert J. Bunker, *Red Teams and Counterterrorism Training*. Norman, OK: University of Oklahoma Press, 2011: 1-160.

Jessica Stern and J. M. Berger, *ISIS: The State of Terror*. New York, NY: HarperCollins, 2015: 1-416.

John P. Sullivan, Ed., *Jane's Unconventional Weapons Handbook*. Alexandria, VA: Jane's Information Group, 2000: 1-315.

Mark A. Tallman, *Ghost Guns: Hobbyists, Hackers, and the Homemade Weapons Revolution*. Santa Barbara, CA: Praeger, 2020: 1-180.

Truls Hallberg Tønnessen, "**Islamic State and Technology – A Literature Review**." *Perspectives on Terrorism*. Vol. 11, No. 6, 2017: 101-111.

Anthony Tu, *Chemical and Biological Weapons and Terrorism*. Boca Raton, FL: CRC Press, 2017: 1-195.

Yannick Veilleux-Lepage, *How Terror Evolves: The Emergence and Spread of Terrorist Techniques*. Lanham, MD: Rowman & Littlefield, 2020: 1-198.

Jacob Ware, "**Terrorist Groups, Artificial Intelligence, and Killer Drones**." *War on the Rocks*. 24 September 2019.

J. Kenneth Wickiser et al., "**Engineered Pathogens and Unnatural Biological Weapons: The Future Threat of Synthetic Biology**." *CTC Sentinel*. Vol. 13, Iss. 8. August 2020: 1-7.

Printed in the United States
By Bookmasters